38

Social History of Canada

H.V. Nelles, general editor

Banking en français: The French Banks of Quebec, 1835–1925

Ronald Rudin provides the first historical examination of franco-phone participation within a particular sector of the economy. By examining the operations of the French-run chartered banks from the establishment of the Banque du Peuple in 1835 to the emergence of the Banque Canadienne Nationale.in 1925, he challenges various notions regarding the role of French-speakers in the economy. The operations of the nine French banks which functioned during this period provided little evidence that French-speaking businessmen were fearful of success, were poor judges of markets, or were reluctant to take risks.

These banks operated in a manner similar to that of English-run banks of a comparable size. The exception to this rule was in terms of the market from which the French banks drew their funds. The bulk of their shareholders and depositors were French-speaking, as barely a dent was made in the English-speaking market. Indeed, by the early twentieth century the Canadian capital market was clearly fragmented along linguistic lines. Professor Rudin concludes – after examining government and corporate records – that these francophone enterprises were limited not by any lack of business sense among their leaders but by their problems in tapping a larger capital market.

RONALD RUDIN is an associate professor in the Department of History, Concordia University.

RONALD RUDIN

Banking en français: The French Banks of Quebec, 1835–1925

UNIVERSITY OF TORONTO PRESS
Toronto Buffalo London

© University of Toronto Press 1985
Toronto Buffalo London
Printed in Canada

ISBN 0-8020-2560-9 cloth
ISBN 0-8020-6579-1 paper

Canadian Cataloguing in Publication Data

Rudin, Ronald
    Banking en français
    (The Social history of Canada, ISSN 0085-6207; 38)
    Bibliography: p.
    Includes index.
    ISBN 0-8020-2560-9 (bound)   0-8020-6579-1 (pbk.)
    1. Banks and banking – Quebec (Province) – History.
    I. Title. II. Series.
    HG2709.Q4R83 1985   332.1′20′9714   C85-098379-7

Social History of Canada 38

Cover illustration: Courtesy of Currency Museum, Bank of Canada.
Photography by Zagon, Ottawa

TO MY PARENTS

Contents

TABLES, FIGURE, AND MAP   viii

PREFACE   ix

1 Introduction   3
2 Beginnings: 1835–75   22
3 Hard Times: 1875–1900   46
4 The Small-town Banks: 1873–1908   78
5 The Survivors: 1900–21   97
6 The Establishment of the Banque Canadienne Nationale:
   1921–5   119
7 Conclusion   141

APPENDICES
1 Operations of the Quebec Banks: 1857–1925   151
2 Data Regarding Shareholders: 1871–1921   154
3 Directors of the Quebec Banks: 1817–1925   156
4 Branches of Canadian Banks: 1871–1921   157

NOTES   159

BIBLIOGRAPHY   175

INDEX   183

Tables, Figure, and Map

TABLES

1.1 The French Banks of Quebec, 1835–1925   5

1.2 Ratio of Population to Branches, 1871–1921   8

1.3 English Bank Branches in Quebec, 1871–1921   11

1.4 French Bank Branches in Quebec, 1871–1921   17

2.1 French Banks and French Capital, 1871–1921   30

3.1 Liquidity of Quebec Banks with Total Assets of $5–10 Million, 30 June 1899   67

3.2 French Investment in the French Banks, 1871–1901   77

4.1 Local Capital and the Small-Town Banks, 1901   79

5.1 Selected Assets of the French Banks, January 1921   102

5.2 Advances of Over $100,000 by Sector   107

5.3 Savings Deposits as a Percentage of Total Liabilities: Quebec Banks, 1919   117

6.1 Liquid Assets of Banque d'Hochelaga and Banque Nationale, 30 November 1923   134

7.1 Francophone Investors and the French Banks, 1871–1921   143

7.2 Selected Occupations of the Directors of the Quebec Banks, 1835–1925   143

A.1 Banque Nationale, 1861   155

FIGURE

6.1 Banque Nationale, Total Deposits by Public, 1921–3   122

MAP

2.1 Quebec Cities Possessing Bank Head Offices   38

Preface

It is only in the last decade that historians have begun to take French-Canadian businessmen and their firms seriously. This new approach was evident in Gerald Tulchinsky's *The River Barons*, in which francophone businessmen were given a significant role to play in the Montreal economy of the mid-nineteenth century.[1] Similarly, in his *Maisonneuve* Paul-André Linteau highlighted the promotional skills of a group of French-speaking businessmen in the development of a Montreal industrial suburb.[2] But while both of these works touch upon the businesses of certain francophone entrepreneurs, neither claims to be a history of francophone enterprise. Lengthy studies of French-controlled firms exist only in the form of authorized histories or unpublished theses.[3] As for a history of French-Canadian participation within a single sector of the economy, none exists.

What follows is an analysis of the role of francophones within the Canadian banking industry. The focus is upon banking partly because of the interest that has been generated in the role of the banks in Canadian economic development by Tom Naylor's *History of Canadian Business*.[4] Moreover, banking offers a typical example of a sector in which francophone participation has been either scorned or ignored. In his history of Canadian banking, R.M. Breckenridge could find nothing more significant to say about the operations of the French banks than to pay reference to

their alleged role in the rebellions of 1837.[5] For his part, Adam
Shortt referred to them only in terms of their occasional need to
suspend operations.[6] More recently, Naylor minimized their
significance, seeing them as 'small Québécois-dominated institutions with local roots in small urban centres or Montreal
suburbs.'[7] In the French literature the francophone banks have
only been dealt with at length in one journal article, one official
history, and three theses, two completed and one nearing completion as this manuscript is being prepared.[8]

This, then, is an institutional history of the French banks from
the establishment of the Banque du Peuple in 1835 to the emergence of the Banque Canadienne Nationale in 1925. The Banque
du Peuple was the first French bank, while the creation of the
Banque Canadienne Nationale (BCN) ushered in a period of
corporate stability among the French banks that was to last until
the BCN's merger with the Banque Provinciale to create the Banque Nationale du Canada in 1979. But from the start the phrase
'French bank' was one that had its ambiguities. On the one hand,
the Banque du Peuple has generally been considered 'French'
even though the bulk of its stock was owned by English-speaking
individuals through its history. On the other hand, the Banque
Internationale, which operated briefly during the 1910s under the
leadership of Sir Rodolphe Forget, is normally not included in
this category despite the fact that most of its capital was controlled by French-speakers.

This study of nine of Canada's chartered banks will include the
Banque du Peuple and exclude the Banque Internationale: the
institutions chosen for this study were united by more than stock
ownership. All nine, including the Banque du Peuple, emerged
because of the recognition by certain French businessmen that
better banking services were necessary to assist their enterprises.
As the histories of these banks unfolded, they often required
English capital to expand and occasionally were even taken over
by English interests. But what they maintained from the start was
an expectation that their clientele was to be found in francophone
Quebec. This was largely true of the people that bought their
stock, and overwhelmingly true of those that deposited funds
and applied for credit. The Banque Internationale, by contrast,

was heavily dependent upon European sources of capital and saw its dealings, as its name implied, to be of a transatlantic nature.

The role of ethnicity was central to the emergence of the French banks and to their continued existence in 1925. After all, most of Canada's smaller banks had passed from the scene by that date, and the French banks might have experienced the same fate had it not been for their control over the savings of francophone Quebecers. It would be incorrect, however, to see this as a study of a group of banks that were untouched by larger developments taking place within the Canadian banking system and within the Canadian economy. It has often been the mistake of those who have studied francophone enterprise to assume that it operated under entirely different pressures from those experienced by comparable English firms. In fact, the French banks were established by merchants who differed only in language from the English-speakers who formed the smaller banks of Quebec. Moreover, the same forces that led to the disappearance of most of the smaller English banks also depleted the ranks of French institutions. And during their years of operation the evolution of the structure of bank assets and liabilities among the French banks largely paralleled the changes experienced by English banks of a comparable size.

While the forces that affected the French banks were largely the same ones that influenced institutions operating in English, the role of ethnicity was always there, interacting with the changing structure of the economy to influence the operations of the French banks. For instance, while all of Canada's smaller banks faced considerable difficulties during the early 1900s, the French ones were limited in their ability to respond to the challenge of monopoly capitalism. Some of the English banks were simply swept from the scene, while others managed to expand their operations so as to try to compete with the giants of the industry, but there were few options for the French institutions. Two of them continued to survive because of their lock on the francophone Quebec market, but they were unable to expand to any great degree because of their inaccessibility to English markets.

The fortunes of the French banks were determined both by the changing structure of the Canadian economy and by the linguistic fragmentation that existed within Canadian banking. These twin forces occupy centre stage in this analysis of the history of the French banks. Following an introductory chapter, which describes the environment in which these institutions operated, there are five chapters that proceed in a roughly chronological order to trace the development of the banks. The institutional bias of the study should be apparent from the manner in which a number of banks are considered in succession within each of these chapters. In these five chapters, and more particularly in the concluding chapter, there are discussions of changes that took place within the Quebec economy as well as within Quebec society. Nevertheless, my principal preoccupation has been to understand the operations of these banks and the environment in which they operated. The role of banks in directing the course of the Canadian economy, which has been of central concern to other authors, is not my major focus here.

The emphasis in this study is upon viewing the French banks as institutions that reflected the environment in which they operated and not as agents that structured that environment. This is not to say that the banks were insignificant players in shaping the economy, but I have not adopted such an approach because the evidence that might convincingly isolate the influence of the banks in the process of economic change is lacking. For instance, one might assert that the French banks played a major role either in encouraging or retarding the agricultural development of Quebec, but in either case the lack of evidence would reduce such claims to the level of speculation. By contrast, because of the close links between the French banks and the Quebec market it is eminently possible to see these banks as reflectors of changes that occurred in that environment. Clearly, the French banks established numerous branches in rural Quebec in the late nineteenth and early twentieth centuries to mobilize savings that had become available, regardless of the precise cause for their appearance. For an institutional study such as this, understanding the characteristics of the environment in which the French banks operated has been of primary importance.

As befits an institutional study of this type, much of the documentation comes from the banks under examination. Because of a number of corporate reorganizations, the records of five of the banks under study here have ended up in the vaults of the Banque Nationale du Canada (BNC), the one remaining French bank. While an invaluable source of information, these records provide considerably more information about bank operations in the twentieth century than they do about the nineteenth, and for certain issues, such as the interest rates offered on savings, the documentation is fragmentary for the entire period under study. The records of a sixth bank, the Banque de St-Hyacinthe, are in the Archives Nationales du Québec in Montreal. No trace could be found, however, of the records of the Banque Ville-Marie, the Banque de St-Jean, or the Banque du Peuple. The absence of detailed information about the last bank, the sole French entry in Canadian banking between 1835 and 1860, means that the treatment of that period is more cursory than I would have liked.

The period prior to 1857 also suffers from the absence of regular monthly reports from the banks to the Canadian government. Even when available, these reports, which are crucial to an analysis of the structure of bank assets and liabilities, present some methodological difficulties. These problems are discussed in the first appendix, which also deals with data regarding bank profits and dividends. Subsequent appendices discuss the way in which information regarding shareholders, directors, and bank branches was manipulated. In addition to these statistical sources, this study also leans upon several collections in the Public Archives, most notably the papers of the finance department, and upon manuscript collections housed in archives from Toronto to Halifax, as well as upon the culling of information from numerous newspapers and business journals.

All of the sources available were not used exhaustively. Had I decided to try to analyse all of the documentation in the archives of the BNC, I would still be there. Similarly, I have not tried to answer all of the questions that this study might raise. I hope that this volume provides a clear description of the operations and the limitations of the French banks. If it raises questions about francophone enterprise in a new light, then my effort was successful.

Limited as this effort might be in certain respects, it could never have been completed without assistance from various quarters. This project was aided financially over several years by sshrc general research funds supplied through Concordia University. During 1982–3 the manuscript was completed with the support of research grants from both the sshrc and fcac, the Quebec government's agency for support of academic research. Most of this money went to support an excellent group of research assistants who aided in the collection of the statistical data. My special thanks go to Isabelle St-Martin, Peter Gossage, Sandra Steiman, Peter Deslauriers, and Francesca Worrall. I also have to thank the Concordia University Computer Centre, which tolerated my large monthly bills when my funds were limited. Kevin O'Connor of the computer centre was particularly patient with my frequent problems in comprehending the mysteries of the system. I also appreciate the tolerance of Glenn Wright of the Public Archives, Jules Jobin of the Banque Nationale du Canada, and Freeman Clowery of the Bank of Montreal, all of whom put large amounts of documentation at my disposal over a number of years. In more general terms, I should also thank the Banque Nationale, without whose co-operation the project could not have existed. Last, but not least, my thanks to my wife Phyllis for her patience with me during the years of this project and for her talents as an editor. She has now heard more about banks than she ever wants to hear and still wonders why we are not rich if I think I know so much about high finance.

This book has been published with the help of a grant from the Social Science Federation of Canada, using funds provided by the Social Sciences and Humanities Research Council of Canada, and a grant from the Andrew W. Mellon Foundation to the University of Toronto Press.

Head office of the Banque du Peuple (*Revue Canadienne*, 1895)

Louis-Michel Viger and Jacob DeWitt, two of the founders of the Banque du Peuple (*Revue Canadienne*, 1895)

Jacques Grenier, president of
the Banque du Peuple, 1885–95
(Archives de la Ville de Montréal)

Head office of the Banque Nationale (Annual Report of the Banque Nationale, 1912)

Interior of the head office of the Banque Nationale (Annual Report of the Banque Nationale, 1912)

Banque Nationale branch in Paris (Annual Report of the Banque
Nationale, 1912)

Banque Nationale, Montreal branch (Annual Report of the Banque
Nationale, 1912)

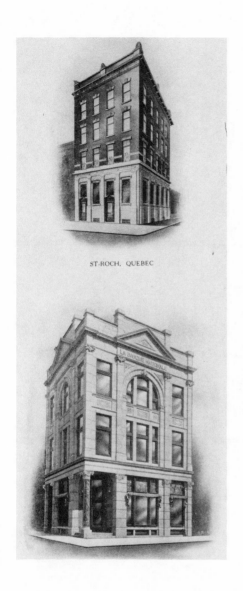

ST-ROCH, QUEBEC

Banque Nationale, branches in St-Roch (Quebec City) and Trois-Rivières (Annual Report of the Banque Nationale, 1912)

Head office of the Banque Jacques-Cartier (*Canadian Illustrated News*, 7 June 1873)

J.-L. Beaudry, president of the
Banque Jacques-Cartier, 1861–9
and 1876–8 (*Canadian Illustrated
News*, 7 April 1877)

Alphonse Desjardins, president
of the Banque Jacques-Cartier,
1878–99 (Public Archives of
Canada, PA-27753)

William Weir, president of the
Banque Ville-Marie, 1881–99
(Notman Photographic Archives,
McCord Museum, McGill
University)

Georges-Casimir Dessaulles,
president of the Banque de St-
Hyacinthe, 1878–1908 (Public
Archives of Canada, PA-49812)

F.-X. St-Charles, president of
the Banque d'Hochelaga, 1879–
1909 (Notman Photographic
Archives, McCord Museum,
McGill University)

F.-L. Béïque, vice-president of
the Banque d'Hochelaga/Banque
Canadienne Nationale, 1912–28;
president of the Banque
Canadienne Nationale, 1928–33
(Notman Photographic Archives,
McCord Museum, McGill
University)

Four bank notes from various French banks (Courtesy of Currency Museum, Bank of Canada; photography by Zagon, Ottawa)

BANKING EN FRANÇAIS

1

Introduction

To many observers Place d'Armes, in the heart of Old Montreal, must add substance to the belief that in the nineteenth century the leaders of French and English Canada subscribed to different sets of values. To the north of the square one finds the imposing head office of the Bank of Montreal, from whose boardrooms major projects such as the building of the CPR were plotted. Across the square, past the monument to Montreal's founder Maisonneuve, is Notre Dame Basilica, representing the conservative, Catholic, and anti-business ideas allegedly held by the francophone elite.[1] That things have changed only recently might appear evident from the gleaming skyscraper of the Banque Nationale du Canada, which occupies the west side of the square.

Just to the east of Place d'Armes on rue St-Jacques sits a building whose history spoils the neat division of the English and the French into two separate camps. The building in question is now no more than a burnt-out shell, but it once housed the head offices of the Banque du Peuple, the first French bank. Opened for business in 1894, this building was much hailed, for the bank moved in at the same time it was about to celebrate its sixtieth anniversary. As one journal noted, 'La nouvelle construction est un véritable triomphe pour les architectes et les constructeurs canadiens-français ... La salle où sont maintenant les bureaux de la banque est exceptionnellement vaste et tout y respire l'élégance et le bon goût.'²

While the Banque du Peuple was the first French bank established in the nineteenth century,⁺it was hardly the last. Between 1835 and 1875 seven chartered banks which were run and largely financed by francophones were established. All of the French banks that have functioned to this day can trace their roots to these seven, which emerged as part of a general expansion of competition within the Canadian banking industry. While only eleven chartered banks existed in British North America at the start of 1835, the number of banks in operation in Canada reached an all-time high of fifty-one by 1875. This expansion was largely fuelled by the desire on the part of merchants who operated on a reasonably modest scale to create regionally based institutions that might facilitate their businesses. The larger banks such as the Bank of Montreal were generally in the business of aiding the movement of staples from Upper Canada to Britain with the result that internal commerce was largely being ignored. The men who started institutions like the Banque du Peuple were in fact no different from those involved in the formation of the Ontario Bank in Bowmanville in 1859 or the Exchange Bank of Yarmouth, Nova Scotia in 1869.

During the half-century between 1875 and 1925, the amount of competition both within the Canadian banking industry and within the economy in general was greatly reduced. The larger banks came to see the advantage of using their unlimited power to establish branches so as to mobilize the savings of Canadians and to give themselves a new source of loanable funds. In the process, the banks, which controlled over half of all financial intermediary assets throughout this period, hoped to halt the decline of their share of these assets to the mortgage loan and insurance companies. By 1921 savings deposits represented nearly half of all bank liabilities, a far cry from the 22% in 1881. Typical was the case of the Bank of Montreal which had only 46 branches as late as 1901, a number which reached 335 by 1921. In the process savings deposits, which accounted for only 35% of the Bank of Montreal's total liabilities in 1901, increased to 45% two decades later.³

TABLE 1.1
The French banks, 1835–1925.

Bank	Location of head office	Year opened	Year closed	Cause for closing
Banque du Peuple	Montreal	1835	1895	Liquidated
Banque Nationale	Quebec	1860	1924	Purchased by Banque d'Hochelaga
Banque Jacques-Cartier	Montreal	1862	1900	Reorganized as Banque Provinciale
Banque Ville-Marie	Montreal	1872	1899	Liquidated
Banque de St-Jean	St-Jean	1873	1908	Liquidated
Banque d'Hochelaga	Monreal	1874	1925	Name changed to Banque Canadienne Nationale
Banque de St-Hyacinthe	St-Hyacinthe	1874	1908	Liquidated
Banque Provinciale	Montreal	1900	1979	Merged to create Banque Nationale du Canada
Banque Canadienne Nationale	Montreal	1925	1979	

As the larger banks spread their branches across the country, they came into conflict with the institutions that had been established by the local merchants. These smaller banks were placed in an uncompetitive position and were either forced out of existence or acquired by the titans of the industry. By the end of 1925 only eleven banks were still in operation, and of these eleven, only three remained whose businesses were of a regional nature. The tiny Weyburn Security Bank only lasted until 1931, but the two surviving French banks, the Banque Canadienne Nationale and the Banque Provinciale, continued on until their merger in 1979.

The survival of two of the French banks was indicative of the fact that banking services had evolved in a very different manner in francophone Quebec from that which had been evident in English Canada. In the rest of the country the disappearance of the smaller banks led to the staging of a major public-relations drive by the industry's apologists, who had the job of explaining why the movement of savings from one region to another was a benefit to the region whose funds were being sent elsewhere. Spokesmen such as H.M.P. Eckhardt admitted that this movement of funds was part of a highly centralized system. He noted in 1911, 'Usually it is found that the branches in the farming districts of the eastern provinces show an excess of deposits, while the branches in the eastern cities and manufacturing towns, and the general run of country banks in the western provinces, show an excess of loans and discounts.'[4] Still, Eckhardt argued, the Canadian banking system was one of 'extraordinary merit,' as even the smallest towns had 'decent banking facilities.'[5] Nor was this an insignificant consideration in a system in which gaining credit was nearly impossible without a local bank branch from which the manager might watch over the investment. The point was frequently made that bankless towns were common in the United States, but all but non-existent in Canada by the early twentieth century.[6]

These arguments, however, had relatively little meaning in Quebec, where the bankless town was still very much in existence in 1921. While only three towns in all of English Canada with populations of 1,000 to 5,000 lacked a bank branch in 1921, there were thirty-one such towns in Quebec.[7] These towns represented over one-quarter of all communities in that category in the province. Nor was this lack of banking facilities something new, as in earlier years even larger Quebec towns had been in this situation. In 1871, for instance, of the three Quebec centres with populations of between 5,000 and 10,000 only one possessed a branch, as did only four of the eight towns in this category in 1881. Ten years later Lévis, with a population of over 7,000, was the largest bankless town in Canada. If a town did not have a branch, it was not always a simple proposition for residents to go to a neighbouring town for banking services. Quebec not only had bankless towns, it also had bankless regions. In 1891, for instance, the Quebec portion of the Ottawa Valley, the areas to the north and south of Quebec City, and the Saguenay–Lac St-Jean regions were all without banking services, leaving over 350,000 people in the cold.

Even when Quebec communities received banking services, they tended to be well below the norm for comparable towns elsewhere in Canada. In 1871, for instance, if one excludes towns which were bankless, there were 4,394 Quebecers per branch in towns with populations of 5,000 to 10,000, while the comparable figure for Canada as a whole was 3,276. Fifty years later, following the expansion of branch banking, the same situation still existed. In towns of 1,000 to 5,000 residents, there were nearly 1,400 Quebecers for each branch and only 1,156 for the country as a whole. This level of service where branches existed, together with the constant presence of the bankless towns, gave Quebec the poorest ratio of population to branches of any province from 1871 to 1911, while in 1921 Quebec only managed to reach eighth place. The Canadian Bankers' Association (CBA) was fond of publishing these ratios for Canada as a whole so as to convince Canadians that their banking system was the best. In 1922 the CBA concluded that Canada's ratio was lower than that of any 'leading Anglo-Saxon country.'[8] But the association was less eager to produce provincial data that would have shown Quebec's place in the system.

Nor was the burden of this level of service borne equally by

TABLE 1.2
Ratio of population to branches, 1871–1921

	1871	1881	1891	1901	1911	1921
Canada	22,093	14,660	11,646	7,512	3,330	2,085
Prince Edward Island	23,505	9,889	13,634	10,326	6,248	2,215
Nova Scotia	19,390	11,907	8,831	5,050	4,644	3,136
New Brunswick	35,669	24,710	9,735	8,714	5,414	3,315
Quebec	41,068	30,887	22,553	13,627	6,307	3,189
Ontario	15,890	10,645	9,153	6,655	2,931	1,880
Manitoba	*	10,376	11,731	4,815	2,606	1,794
Saskatchewan	*	*	*	9,128	1,777	1,281
Alberta	*	*	*	4,868	1,990	1,421
British Columbia	12,082	16,486	10,908	4,060	2,515	2,176

*Ratio could not be calculated, owing to either an absence of branches or a lack of population data.
Source: See appendix IV.

French- and English-speaking Quebecers. For instance, among the towns that were bankless in 1921, over three-quarters had populations which were more than 75% of French origin. In that same year among towns with banking services and populations of between 1,000 and 5,000 there were 950 Quebecers per branch in towns less than 25% French, while at the other end of the spectrum there were over 1,450 Quebecers per branch in towns more than 75% French. Throughout the half-century following Confederation, the bankless town was almost unheard-of among predominantly English communities and when banking services were available for English and French towns of a comparable size, the former generally received better service.

It is difficult, if not impossible, to specify what this level of banking services meant to the development of the Quebec economy. Clearly, to the leaders of some towns the absence of banking facilities constituted an obstacle to growth. The archives of Canadian banks, French and English alike, are filled with the petitions that were sent by businessmen from Quebec communities who saw that a branch was essential to their enterprises;

newspapers in many of these towns made the securing of a branch a major cause to pursue in the boosting of the local economy. As the newspaper of one bankless Quebec town noted in 1857, 'Il est certain qu'une banque est une chose absolument nécessaire à St-Hyacinthe. Pour l'importateur, pour le spéculateur, pour l'entrepreneur, pour tous nos marchands, pour tous ceux enfin dont les affaires requièrent des débourses.' The same journal went on to note that 'tant que nous n'aurions pas une banque à St-Hyacinthe il est difficile de compter sur l'établissement de manufactures.'[9]

Whether the arrival of branch banking in St-Hyacinthe only in 1870 retarded the industrial development of the city is difficult to say. Nor is it a simple proposition to link the expansion of banking facilities in the town to the substantial industrial growth experienced during the 1880s and 1890s. There were clearly other factors involved, such as the resource base, the availability of labour and capital, and the nature of government policy. What is clear, however, is that the relatively low level of banking services in Quebec, and more particularly in its francophone areas, provided the French banks with a market in which they could expand during the late nineteenth and early twentieth centuries. Following their establishment by French merchants in need of accommodation, the French banks might have gone the way of the small Maritime banks which had disappeared by the early 1900s, had it not been for the relative failure of the English banks to penetrate the francophone Quebec market. As savings deposits became the chartered banks' major source of loanable funds, the loss of the francophone Quebec market would have doomed the French banks which failed in their attempts to expand into English speaking markets. As the rest of this chapter will indicate, the banking industry evolved in a linguistically fragmented fashion providing the French banks with a raison d'étre.

II

The banks that provided services to Quebec during this period were a diverse lot. There were those banks which operated in

English and others whose language of business was primarily French. Moreover, within each linguistic grouping there were considerable gaps between the largest and smallest institutions. In 1901 the most important of the English banks serving Quebec was the Bank of Montreal with assets of nearly $95 million, while the smallest was the People's Bank of Halifax with less than $4 million. The largest of the French banks, the Banque d'Hochelaga, had total assets of only $10 million, but it still dwarfed the Banque de St-Jean, whose assets were valued at less than $750,000.

In terms of nearly every aspect of the operations of these banks, size was more important than language as a factor influencing their operations. For instance, by 1921 the larger the bank the more likely it was to have issued notes well in excess of its paid capital, to have invested a significant percentage of its assets in stocks and bonds, and to have earned solid profits and declared large dividends.[10] But in terms of where a bank might establish its branches, language was clearly more important than size.

It would be unfair to argue that the English banks ignored Quebec, since they generally operated the majority of branches in the province. Nevertheless, these branches never accounted for more than a small percentage of all English bank branches. Moreover, these offices were highly concentrated in Montreal and Quebec City, and were generally located in towns whose population was more than 5,000 or less than 75% French.[11] Despite a considerable increase in the number of English bank branches in Quebec during the first two decades of the 1900s, the general profile of the Quebec town served by the English banks remained largely the same.

These patterns did not vary greatly among English banks of different size. The Bank of Montreal, for instance, had only three of its 46 branches in Quebec in 1901, one in Quebec City and two in Montreal. By 1921, 56 of its 335 branches were located in Quebec, but the majority were in the province's two largest centres and less than one-third were in towns whose population was more than 75% French. From its base in Sherbrooke the Eastern Townships Bank generally operated a larger number of

TABLE 1.3
English bank branches in Quebec, 1871–1921

	1871	1881	1891	1901	1911	1921
Number	24	27	30	74	263	375
% English branches located:						
a. In Montreal or Quebec City	71	55	53	41	41	41
b. In towns of less than 5,000	22	30	32	45	49	46
c. In towns more than 75% French	4	16	*	38	49	37
% of all Quebec branches operated by English banks	82	61	45	61	71	51
% of all English bank branches located in Quebec	15	10	8	11	13	10

*Data not available
Source: See appendix IV.

branches in Quebec than did the Bank of Montreal. Nevertheless, there were still some similarities in the approach of the two towards the province. In 1911, a year before its acquisition by the Canadian Bank of Commerce, the Eastern Townships Bank had 77 of its 89 branches in the province, but the smallest of Quebec's English banks located the majority of these branches in towns less than 75% French.

Why the English banks established numerous branches in Montreal or Quebec City is not difficult to understand, but their general bypassing of smaller French communities requires explanation since it was a key factor in the relative success and continued existence of the French banks. A reading of the deliberations of the directors of such institutions as the Bank of Montreal, the Molson's Bank, and the Merchants' Bank would lead one to believe that such decisions were made solely on hard economic criteria. Normally, one of the banks would receive a request from local residents or a lead from a friend of the bank regarding the possibility of establishing a branch in a particular locale. Further research would then be carried out by the general manager, one of the directors, or the manager of an existing branch in the area. The directors would then sift through the available information, particularly that pertaining to the level of deposits that might be gained from a rural branch, and then arrive at a hard-headed business decision.

On this basis many Quebec towns did not warrant branches, particularly in the late nineteenth century when there were better prospects available in Ontario. The limited quantity of the savings at the disposal of francophone Quebecers was evident from the repeated difficulties of the French banks to find sources of capital within the French community prior to 1900. This situation is not entirely surprising, as the province's agricultural and industrial base continued to lag behind that of Ontario throughout the last third of the century. The agricultural problems which were visible at the time of the Rebellions of 1837 and which later played a role in the massive migration of Quebecers to New England were still visible in 1871, when the value of Quebec agricultural production was only 45% of that of Ontario; despite the appearance of newer forms of farming in certain regions dependent upon dairy production, roughly the same relationship between the value of output in the two provinces still existed in 1901.[12] Similarly, the value of Quebec's industrial production stood at roughly two-thirds of that of Ontario in both 1871 and 1901. Moreover, Quebec industrial production was concentrated in Montreal to a far greater degree than was Ontario's in Toronto.[13] Under these circumstances few Quebec centres could emerge as either agricultural service towns or hives of industry, with the result that there were twenty-eight Ontario towns with more than 5,000 residents in 1901 while there were only ten in Quebec. In addition, one can easily imagine that in the smaller centres of the two provinces there were more business opportunities in Ontario than in Quebec.

Market considerations such as these undoubtedly limited the number of Quebec towns that could hope to secure services from banks which saw all of Canada as their field of operation. But in spite of this generally gloomy picture of pre-1900 Quebec as a whole, there were still serious opportunities for the English banks that remained curiously untouched. Lévis, for instance, located directly across the St Lawrence from Quebec City, was the service centre for the large area to the south because of its location on the river and its excellent railway connections. The town experienced an increase in the value of its industrial production by 80% during the 1880s, but it still remained bankless in 1891. The Merchants' Bank, for example, managed to bypass Lévis and to remain at the Ontario town of Ingersoll even though its directors had noted in 1880 that 'the business is small and must be so as long as there are three branches in Ingersoll a town only large enough for two.'[14]

There was also business to be done in areas such as the plain to the south of Montreal, where agricultural production increased between 1871 and 1901 at a rate well above the provincial norm. That this was the centre of dairy farming in the province was symbolized by the establishment of the provincial government's dairy school at St-Hyacinthe in 1892. As a result of this transformation there were deposits to be found which were seized upon by the Banque du Peuple as it established ten branches between 1885 and its suspension in 1895 that helped it to increase its deposits by over 400%. Particularly profitable was its branch located in the region at St-Rémi, which was yielding deposits of $110,000 in 1895 in spite of a population of barely more than 1,000.[15] When the Banque du Peuple closed, none of the English banks showed any interest in St-Rémi. Rather, the Banque de St-Jean moved in, and in the process increased its deposits by 50% during 1895 alone. In the following year the Merchants' Bank's annual report made reference to 'the silent revolution in Quebec agriculture,' but there was little evidence that this was anything more than lip service.[16]

After the turn of the century the absolute number of English bank branches in the province increased in response to the dramatic change in Quebec's economic fortunes. Between 1901 and 1921 the value of agricultural production in Quebec increased by 478% as opposed to 200% in Ontario.[17] In addition, rural Quebec was transformed through the exploitation of new natural resources, most notably hydroelectricity, which in its turn was central to the growth of the pulp and paper industry. More traditional industrial sectors such as the manufacturing of textile and tobacco products also increased in importance, with the result that the value of industrial production in constant dollars more than doubled between 1901 and 1921.[18]

In spite of these changes, the English banks continued to operate only a small percentage of their Quebec branches in small francophone towns, even though these communities were often the beneficiaries of the province's growth. Take, for instance, the case of the town of St-Césaire, located near St-Hyacinthe. At the start of 1908 it was served only by the Banque de St-Hyacinthe, which had collected deposits exceeding $180,000.[19] When the Banque de St-Hyacinthe suspended operations later in the same year, the Bank of Montreal moved into St-Césaire, but it stayed open for only one week before giving way to the Banque Provinciale.[20] This departure is particularly interesting since the deposits available at St-Césaire were superior to the minimum level of $175,000 set by the Bank of Montreal for the opening of new branches.[21]

Actions such as these suggest that there may have been more than a simple reading of the balance sheet dictating the operations of the English banks in Quebec. Suggestions that credit-worthy French clients were denied support by those English branches that were established in the province were certainly common in the French press. For instance, *Le Prix Courant* was convinced that there was little chance of francophones receiving support from the Coaticook branch of the Eastern Townships Bank. It noted, 'Nos compatriotes commerçants se trouvent là, comme à Montréal et ailleurs, dans un état d'infériorité vis-à-vis leurs concurrents de langue anglaise pour qui la banque a des complaisances qu'elle refuse aux nôtres.'[22]

The available information does not permit an analysis of the lending policies of the English banks, to show whether comparable English and French clients were treated in a similar fashion. Nevertheless, some comments made by leaders of these banks tend to support the claims of unequal treatment. The Merchants' Bank, for instance, told one of its better customers, a Montreal importer and wholesaler, that it would be pleased to discount 'that portion of his account which represents his dealings with English speaking customers ... Objection would not be taken to an account with one of the French banks for the negotiation of French Canadian paper.'[23] Ultimately, the client reached an agreement for 'ses transactions de banque avec sa clientèle canadienne-française' with the Banque Jacques-Cartier, but lacking such an arrangement the client's dealings with francophone retailers would have been in jeopardy, apparently for no other reason than their mother tongue.[24] The sentiment of the Merchants' Bank was also reflected by the cashier of the Bank of Nova Scotia who complained during an inspection of the bank's recently opened branch in Montreal that there was 'too much French about it.'[25]

It would appear that the English banks were often less than enthusiastic about dealing with French clients in centres with numerous English customers such as Montreal. Accordingly, there was little reason why they should have gone out of their way to establish themselves in the exclusively French towns of the province. The Bank of Nova Scotia only reluctantly opened at Quebec City when the Quebec Gas Company was acquired by a Toronto syndicate with which it was connected, but these English business opportunities were not always present.[26] The same bank considered going into Berthierville until the town's major English firm agreed to do business with another bank. The general manager concluded that there was then no reason for 'the establishment of a branch in a French section.'[27]

The factors that inhibited the English banks from establishing more offices in the province's French communities were undoubtedly numerous, and must have varied from banker to banker. Some may have suspected that anyone who spoke French was by definition a bad risk, while others may have had a residual impression that Quebec was an area of little economic vitality in spite of the changes that took place during this period, and particularly after 1900. To many this reluctance was probably also linked to a lack of information about potential locations and clients. Without such information the perceived risk of any transaction increased, and the reduction of risk was central to the actions of a good banker. One could not really have expected these men to have had much information on the French community, for few of their directors or major shareholders were French. When Lomer Gouin was appointed to the board of directors of the Bank of Montreal in 1920, he was the first francophone to have held such a position since the 1840s. Nor is this surprising when it is realized that only 4% of Bank of Montreal stock was held by francophones in 1921, a situation that was similar to that of other English banks.[28] But whatever the precise reasons for the actions, or inaction, of the English banks in the overwhelmingly francophone regions of Quebec may have been, this behaviour was central both to the level of banking services available in the province and to the continued existence of a number of French-controlled banks which tried to fill the void.[29]

III

Observers of the Quebec business scene were not unaware of the opportunities for expansion that were left to the French banks by the English bankers. In 1888 a correspondent to *Le Prix Courant* stated the obvious, noting that the Bank of Montreal 'néglige complètement notre province et réserve toutes ses faveurs au Haut Canada.' He was not in the least dismayed by this situation because 'heureusement, nos banques canadiennes[-françaises] ont entrepris de combler cette lacune.'[30] Another journal expressed the same sentiment on the sixtieth anniversary of the founding of the Banque du Peuple. Instead of crushing French enterprise, the policies of the English banks had given the French institutions a field in which to operate. 'Un politique moins haineuse, moins étroitement égoïste aurait probablement reculé de beaucoup l'établissement de nos banques canadiennes-françaises: A quelque chose, malheur est bon.'[31]

Aware that there were markets to conquer, several of the French banks agressively expanded their branch systems in the late nineteenth century, invariably situating their offices in Quebec towns whose populations were predominantly French.

TABLE 1.4
French bank branches in Quebec, 1871–1921

	1871	1881	1891	1901	1911	1921
Number	5	17	36	47	107	365
% French branches located:						
a. In otherwise bankless towns	0	35	47	55	55	36
b. In towns of less than 5,000	0	41	50	57	63	61
c. In towns more than 75% French	25	56	*	78	83	70
% of all Quebec branches operated by French banks	17	39	54	39	29	49
% of all French bank branches located in Quebec	100	94	90	93	92	77

*Data not available
Source: appendix IV

The success of the Banque du Peuple along these lines has already been noted, but equally opportunistic was the Banque Ville-Marie, which increased its number of branches from one in 1881 to twenty in 1899 on the eve of its suspension of operations. Fourteen of these were situated outside Montreal, and all were located in small Quebec towns with populations which were more than 75% French. By 1899 the bank's deposits reached $1.25 million, and it was described as having 'drawn more small capital from the farming community of the province than any other bank.'[32]

The expansionist policies of the Banque du Peuple and the Banque Ville-Marie helped the French banks temporarily to hold the majority of branches in the province in the early 1890s. However, by the end of the century both had disappeared – not because of their failure to mobilize savings in rural Quebec, but rather because of the poor management of these funds. In fact, the savings in the coffers of these and other French banks of the era might have been even greater had it not been for their chronic lack of capital, a symptom often referred to in the French business press of the time. This lack of capital is testified to by the frequent infusion of English capital whenever expansion was attempted. Moreover, it was reflected in the unwillingness of the Banque Ville-Marie to 'waste' any of its branches in towns served by one of the other French banks. This was the case in 1894 when the Ville-Marie closed its branch in Louiseville upon the arrival of the Banque d'Hochelaga. The president of the former bank, William Weir, never indicated that Louiseville could not support two banks. Rather, his concern was that scarce resources would be wasted in competition with another bank, when bankless towns waited to be served. Weir calculated that there were 135 centres with banking services in Ontario and only 41 in Quebec. Accordingly, upon leaving Louiseville, his bank set up shop in the bankless towns of L'Epiphanie and Lachute.[33]

Into the early twentieth century the French banks continued to draw deposits from an essentially francophone Quebec market. The three banks that operated throughout the first quarter of the century, the Banque Nationale, the Banque Provinciale, and the Banque d'Hochelaga, functioned on a much more solid basis than had the French banks during the nineteenth century, owing to the greater capital at the disposal of certain francophones in a period of economic growth in Quebec. Between 1901 and 1921 the total capital of the three increased from $3.45 to $8 million with nearly all the new funds coming from francophones. Accordingly, by 1921 the capital market within the banking industry had become highly fragmented along linguistic lines with 97% of all capital invested by English-speakers going to English banks and 89% of the francophone investment going to the French ones.[34]

This fragmentation was reinforced by the three French banks as they established over 250 new branches in the province between 1901 and 1921. The banks increased their savings deposits by 1100% over this period, twice the figure for the industry as a whole, by zeroing in on the French market. For instance, the Banque Provinciale was enthusiastic about its prospects in Windsor Mills, where 'l'élément anglais fait des affaires et dépose avec la Banque de Commerce. Tout semble converger vers notre institution, quant à la question de race pour les dépôts, parce qu'on parle le français ici.'[35] The same bank avoided a neighbourhood in Montreal where 'considerable changes [had] taken place in the population, mainly Jews and foreigners from which no effective support [could] be expected.'[36]

In spite of the establishment of a large number of new offices by the French banks, numerous Quebec towns that warranted banking services remained bankless in 1921. That these towns could have supported bank branches was evident from the deposits collected by two new types of institutions that emerged upon the scene in the early twentieth century, the caisse populaire and the subagency. The first was the idea of Alphonse Desjardins, a former recorder of the debates in the House of Commons, who wanted to establish co-operative savings banks in each parish of the province. Desjardins believed that the chartered banks, French and English alike, were evil institutions that drained funds from a community while providing little in return. But while Desjardins called for the establishment of caisses populaires to compete with the banks, they invariably took root in the communities which were bankless and which were looking for an agency which might collect their savings at interest. Appropriately, Lévis, a town with a long history of banklessness, was the site of the first caisse in 1901, and by 1921 over 75% of the more than one hundred caisses were in bankless towns.

In 1921 the caisses held total deposits worth $4.5 million, a rather small amount compared to the $135 million in the coffers of the three French banks. Nevertheless, the banks feared that this might be only the tip of the iceberg and that their lock on the savings of francophone Quebecers might be in danger. As one Banque Nationale director noted in 1922, 'If co-operative banks were established on a large scale, they would end by taking a considerable amount from the bank. Until now the amount has been very small. But established on a large scale, they would inevitably lead to the taking of a large portion of the deposits of commercial banks.'[37] These fears were probably fuelled by the fact that the French banks had failed miserably in expanding their operations beyond the francophone market. True, they had successfully implanted themselves in French communities outside

Quebec, so much so that the Banque Provinciale was known informally in the Maritimes as the 'Banque des Acadiens.' But the attempt by the Banque d'Hochelaga to move into English markets in the prairies had been a disaster that one inspector termed 'un insuccès complet.'[38] Accordingly, the caisse populaire threat had to be taken seriously.

Even though several of the rural caisses had collected deposits well in excess of $100,000 by 1921, the French banks did not establish branches to counter Desjardins' challenge.[39] Rather, their response was the opening of 375 subagencies between 1901 and 1921. All Canadian banks operated subagencies which would only open a few days a week as a means of serving small communities that allegedly could not support a regular branch. But while the subagencies operated by the English banks did a regular banking business with a regular staff, the French subagencies did no more than collect deposits. Notaries often served as the banks' agents, and were paid a percentage of the deposits received. As the Banque Provinciale noted, 'No discount or collection is done, no special premises are occupied and no regular staff is employed.'[40]

The leading exponent of the subagency was the Banque Nationale, which is hardly surprising since its competition with the caisses was more intense than that of the other two French banks. In April 1924 over 25% of its total deposits of more than $40 million came from these subagencies, and in numerous cases the deposits received in any one subagency exceeded $100,000, an amount normally sufficient for the Banque Nationale to have opened a branch.[41] But in the manner in which banking services evolved in Quebec, the Banque Nationale and the other French banks were under no pressure to provide full banking services to these towns. The English banks generally were not serious competitors, and the caisses offered little competition in terms of the credit they might offer, as their constitutions discouraged the granting of all but the smallest loans and limited the application of loans to a very few purposes. In this context, the French banks could be confident that francophone Quebecers would have to come to them for full-service banking, and the subagencies provided a sensible means of combating the loss of savings to the caisses. In all, the caisses and the subagencies were serving 383 communities that were otherwise bankless in 1921. The lack of banking services in these towns was one element in Quebec's poor ratio of population to bank branches.

IV

This was the environment in which the French banks evolved. On the one hand, the French bankers shared with their English counterparts certain concerns about the general direction of the industry. Bankers, French and English alike, kept a keen eye on the Bank Act to see that it did not compromise their affairs, and they increasingly worried about the liquidity of their assets as they became ever more dependent upon deposits as a source of loanable funds. But in addition to these concerns of interest to all in the industry, the French bankers had a more specific interest in francophone Quebec because of the fragmentation of the banking market along linguistic lines. The observation made by a group of financiers from France in 1880 held true throughout the period under study. They found that 'several English banks have agencies in the English part of the country while the French Canadian is abandoned to himself.'[42] Accordingly, French bankers watched with great interest changes that took place in the Quebec economy that could mean a greater accessibility to both capital and savings deposits. They also jealously guarded the market that the English banks had abandoned to them. They could not have been pleased that their attempts to crack the English market invariably failed; but the French bankers could at least rest assured that they would be spared the invasion of their turf by the giants of the industry, an invasion that had doomed the smaller banks elsewhere in Canada.

2

Beginnings: 1835–1875

In the aftermath of the Conquest of Quebec by the British in 1760, francophone merchants quickly took a back seat to their English-speaking counterparts in running the economy. The two groups were hardly on an even footing, for the British had imperial connections, customers, and sources of credit in England, as well as access to lucrative military contracts.[1] The French had little more than a knowledge of the operation of the fur trade, a skill of dubious value as the new staples of grain and timber were becoming prominent at the beginning of the nineteenth century.

Historians have generally discussed the fate of the francophone bourgeoisie in terms of the factors that led to its decline following the Conquest. To Michel Brunet this decline was inevitable because the ties to France had been severed, while to Donald Creighton the problem was more one of attitude as francophone society came to be led by men who viewed economic matters 'with an apathy that turned to hatred.'[2] Both views began with the assumption that French participation in the Quebec economy was all but non-existent, but neither allowed for the possibility that while the French had become subservient to the English in economic matters they still played a significant role. Both Brunet and Creighton, in their concentration upon the major merchants involved in the international movement of staples, missed the point that commercial activity took place on various levels. While the English dominated the most lucrative operations, there were nevertheless francophone merchants involved, as were many English merchants, in internal trade.

These varying levels of commercial activity were reflected in the banks established in Canada during the first three-quarters of the nineteenth century. The first banks established in Lower Canada, the Bank of Montreal founded in 1817 and the Quebec Bank which followed a year later, were designed to assist in the movement of staples from Upper Canada to Great Britain. The merchants who petitioned for the chartering of these banks required a circulating medium that they might pay to their suppliers, and so they turned to the government to give them permission to issue bank notes that, redeemable in specie, might enjoy the confidence of the public. They also secured in their charters the right to establish branches wherever they wished, and the guarantee that if their affairs turned out to be completely disastrous creditors would only be able to attach the wealth of the shareholders for an additional amount equal to the value of their investment. Since this last provision had the effect of doubling the shareholders' liability, it is usually referred to as the double liability clause. The state was providing considerable capital for the completion of transportation projects that interested merchants involved in the staple trade, and the granting of these generous conditions for the establishment of banks was a further boon to the merchants.

The merchants who operated on a more modest scale did not find their needs being met by these banks, and they turned to the state for permission to establish institutions of their own. This process, which occurred not only in Quebec but across all of British North America, led to a swelling of the number of banks in operation to an all-time high of 51 by 1875. Francophones played a central part in the movement, establishing seven banks of their own between 1835 and 1875.

This is not to say that francophones were uninvolved in banking prior to 1835. Fully one-third of the directors of the Quebec Bank between 1818 and 1835 were francophones, while the figure was 20% for the City Bank and 10% for the Bank of Montreal.[3] It seems unlikely, however, that these French-speakers held any real power. While the English members of these boards were largely businessmen engaged in international trade, the francophone members were predominantly government officials or professional men who were useful for their political connections, but who had little impact upon decisions regarding bank credit. Creighton was accurate when he noted that the French occupied 'a subordinate part' in the operations of these banks.[4]

This representation by francophone professionals was meaningless to the French merchants who took the first steps towards establishing a bank of their own in 1833, an action that led to the opening of the Banque du Peuple in 1835. Since most historians interested in the years leading up to the Rebellions of 1837 have concentrated their attention upon the actions of Papineau and other members of the liberal professions, hardly any space has been accorded to the actions of these merchants. Not surprisingly, Creighton did not make a single reference to the Banque du Peuple even though it operated for fifteen of the years discussed in his *Empire of the St. Lawrence*; Fernand Ouellet's attention to the bank was hardly more substantial.[5] Between 1850 and 1874 another six French banks came into existence, indicating the increasing assertiveness of this francophone merchant class. The seven French banks in operation at the start of 1875 were to provide the basis for francophone banking to the present.

II

While Creighton may have ignored the Banque du Peuple, those who have discussed its history have done so with a certain amount of exaggeration. The spirit of the discussion was no doubt caused by the fact that this was the first bank in which francophones played a leading role. Thomas Storrow Brown, for instance, was carried away by his enthusiasm for the Banque du Peuple, which he saw as a liberating force for the French population. Brown, who had been a director of the bank from 1835 to 1837, noted, 'The rise of the French element in wealth, business importance and trade in the city since the establishment of the Banque du Peuple ... [is] wonderful to those who can remember their depression up to that time.'[6] This heroic view of the bank was shared by the *Revue Canadienne,* which saw it as central to the 'prospérité commerciale' of the French community.[7]

Such charity was lacking in most English views of the bank, most of which took their inspiration from Lord Durham's claim that the Banque du Peuple helped finance the rebellions of 1837–8. Durham had a few kind words for the bank, noting that its establishment 'by French capitalists is an event which may be regarded as a satisfactory indication of an awakening commercial energy among the French.' But he went on to mourn the fact that 'its success was uniformly promoted by direct and illiberal appeals to the national feelings of race.'[8] The Durham view was carried on by R.M. Breckenridge in his history of Canadian banking published in 1894.[9] Similarly, Adam Shortt wrote that the Banque du Peuple had emerged in spite of the 'blissful ignorance' of the French Canadians of the financial boom of the early 1830s. The bank's 'appearance was significant of political rather than financial unrest.'[10] In other words, the Banque du Peuple was a good idea that had come into being for the wrong reasons.

All of these views, positive and negative alike, tend to ignore the fact that while this bank had an important French element in its direction it was hardly a totally French institution. While its Frenchness made it unique, it was not completely French. That this was a partnership of French and English interests was clear from the first articles for the establishment of the Banque du Peuple de la Cité de Montréal in 1833. These articles, which failed to be implemented, called for the creation of a bank with a capital of £75,000, but less than half of the seventeen names affixed to the proposal were even vaguely French. The causes for the failure of the 1833 scheme are not clear, but six of the original petitioners were back again in 1835 to try once more to form a bank, this time under the title of DeWitt, Viger and Company. The 1835 proposal listed twelve men as provisional directors, seven of whom were French.

If these men were not united by language, they did share a

common political allegiance. As far as can be determined, all of the directors named in both the 1833 and 1835 documents were reform-minded, which is not to say that they necessarily supported a violent solution for the political problems then facing Lower Canada. This political unanimity together with Papineau's 1834 denunciation of the existing banks probably led Durham to see the Banque du Peuple as the financier of the rebellions, a conclusion for which there is no support. But in looking for the political motives behind the bank's emergence, Durham missed the economic ties that united its French and English founders, all of whom were outsiders who did not fit into the world of the Molsons. Louis-Michel Viger and the other French Canadian merchants who promoted the project were clearly outsiders, as was the American Jacob DeWitt, who as early as 1818 had tried to start up a bank for those excluded from the Bank of Montreal clique.[11]

The founders of DeWitt, Viger and Company indicated their own awareness of their role as outsiders when they chose to forego the normal legislative approval for the establishment of a new chartered bank. Such approval was necessary to allow the bank the right to issue notes, but DeWitt, Viger et al. feared that they did not have the necessary political influence to secure a charter and chose instead to operate a private bank. Such banks played an important role in nineteenth-century Canadian banking, with their numbers reaching 138 by 1881.[12] Many of them provided facilities for the deposit and the borrowing of funds in places not served by the chartered banks, but they ultimately disappeared because of the expansion of the branch systems of the chartered banks and their own inability to expand their operations through the issuing of bank notes. DeWitt, Viger and Company circumvented this problem through a legal technicality.[13] The public seemed to accept their notes, which were fittingly 'decorated with the figure of a young habitant,' and the bank survived both the rebellions and the financial panic of 1837.[14] Gerald Tulchinsky has noted that the bank 'entered the forties on a strong financial note' and 'by 1843 had a capital stock worth £200,000.'[15]

The bank also showed itself to be unconventional in its form of organization. All of the chartered banks operated under a system in which a shareholder could be held liable for the debts of the bank up to a limited amount, normally a sum equal to his investment. The directors of the bank, who were annually elected by the shareholders, found themselves in an identical position to that of the ordinary shareholder when it came to paying off the creditors. None of these rules applied to DeWitt, Viger and Company, which was organized as a *société en commandite*. In this structure, the directors were referred to as principal partners, or *associés gérants*, while the shareholders were known as *commanditaires*. From the inception of the bank the principal partners ran the show with little direction from the shareholders. A partner did not have to stand for re-election once he was chosen by the other partners, and as a group the *associés gérants* were required to reveal relatively little of the affairs of the bank to the shareholders at the bank's annual meeting. So secretive were the activities of the partners that the bank's net profits were not revealed until the 1880s. The powerlessness of the ordinary shareholder was made clear in this exchange between the shareholder, F.E. Gilman, and two bank officials at the annual meeting of 1877.

Mr. Gilman: 'I would like to know how much are the working expenses of the Corporation.'
Mr. Trottier (General Manager): 'I don't think the question is in order. That is left with the Corporation' [i.e. the principal partners].
Mr. Gilman: 'So, no one outside these seven gentlemen has the right to know anything about the working expenses.'
Mr. Cherrier (President): 'I must tell you again, that which relates to the administration is entirely out of the power of the stockholders.'[16]

Later in this exchange Gilman was also reminded of the price which the directors of the Banque du Peuple paid for their freedom from scrutiny. The principal partners were, in Cherrier's words, 'responsible for everything,' so that in the case of the failure of the bank they were liable for their entire fortunes while the shareholders could lose no more than their shares in the bank.

As they had relatively little to lose, the shareholders were expected to remain silent.

Despite the various unconventional elements in the establishment of DeWitt, Viger and Company – its Frenchness, its politics, its collection of outsiders, and its form of organization – the firm sought to put itself on an equal footing with the other banks and in 1844 received its charter. The bank became officially known as the Banque du Peuple, although it had unofficially been known by that name from the start. More significantly, the bank gained the right to issue notes. This change indicated that it had gained a certain respectability and lost its notoriety as the financial agent for the Patriotes. In fact, in 1847 the Bank of Montreal, which was moving into new quarters, rented its old building to the Banque du Peuple. The directors of the Bank of Montreal announced that they were 'pleased to have for their neighbours so respectable an institution with which the bank has ever been desirous of cultivating the most friendly relations.'[17]

Both the provincial government and the Bank of Montreal realized by the 1840s that the Banque du Peuple's unorthodox organization was a source of great stability, and not a threat to chartered banking as it then existed. This organization was directly responsible, for instance, for the minimal turnover among the directors of the bank. While shareholders of the other banks were known to purge their directors from time to time, the *associés gérants* were freed from such a fate. Accordingly, the bank had only five presidents from 1835 to 1874, each of whom died in office. Even the bank's cashier, or general manager, B.H. Lemoine, held his post from 1835 to 1870.

In spite of their freedom to do as they pleased, the directors ran the bank's affairs in an extremely conservative fashion. Secrecy did not encourage them to invest bank funds carelessly. Rather, the spectre of unlimited liability for the bank's debts made them particularly cautious. Accordingly, the bank very slowly increased its paid-up capital until it reached its authorized limit of $1.6 million in 1868, and did not seek any increase in this amount during the boom years of the early 1870s when other banks were rapidly increasing their capital. The bank's conservatism was also evident in the slowness with which it sought to expand its operations either through accepting savings deposits or by increasing its note circulation to the level allowed by the government. Accordingly, throughout the pre-1875 period the distribution of the liabilities of the Banque du Peuple was unlike that of any other Quebec-based institution, as the bank was almost entirely dependent upon shareholders' funds to finance its operations. Because of the slowness with which it sought to increase its deposits and expand its note circulation, the Banque du Peuple did not even establish its first branch until the 1880s.[18]

This cautious image must have played a role in perpetuating English investment in a bank that was primarily run by francophone merchants. At the time of the signing of the bank's articles of association an important English presence was evident, and this was still the case in 1871 when roughly two-thirds of bank stock was held by English-speaking interests.[19] With the exception of the Banque Ville-Marie, none of the other French banks ever saw more than 40% of their capital under the control of non-francophones, but the Banque du Peuple was born twenty-five years before the second French bank at a time when investment capital in the French community was not always easy to find. Once this English involvement had begun, there was little reason for it to end, seeing that the directors appeared to be careful money managers.

These directors were overwhelmingly French and primarily engaged in commerce, and in the structure of the Banque du Peuple it was they alone who wielded power.[20] English-speaking investors may have been lured to the bank by the prospect of gaining credit unavailable elsewhere or by the hope of receiving a steady return on their capital; but no matter what their motives may have been, the direction of the bank was set by francophones who looked to a French market for the bank's clientele. Just how dependent the Banque du Peuple was upon the francophone Quebec market became clear when the bank aggressively expanded its operations in the 1880s.

TABLE 2.1
French banks and French capital, 1871–1921

	Value of subscribed capital ($) (% controlled by francophones)					
	1871	1881	1891	1901	1911	1921
Banque du Peuple	1,600,000 (33)	1,600,000 (39)	1,200,000 (41)	–	–	–
Banque Jacques-Cartier/ Banque Provinciale	1,900,350 (75)	500,000 (60)	500,000 (80)	863,387 (88)	1,000,000 (85)	3,000,000 (89)
Banque d'Hochelaga	–	682,060 (88)	710,100 (76)	1,500,000 (74)	2,500,000 (82)	4,000,000 (87)
Banque Ville-Marie	–	1,000,000 (89)	500,000 (73)	–	–	–
Banque Nationale	2,000,000 (71)	2,000,000 (74)	1,200,000 (76)	1,200,000 (90)	2,000,000 (93)	2,000,000 (93)
Banque de St-Hyacinthe	–	504,600 (92)	504,600 (99)	504,600 (98)	–	–
Banque de St-Jean	–	540,000 (93)	500,200 (97)	500,000 (99)	–	–
All French banks	5,509,350 (62)	6,826,660 (65)	5,114,900 (72)	4,568,187 (86)	5,500,000 (86)	9,000,000 (89)

Sources: Canadian Sessional Papers, 1871–1911; PAC, RG14, D2, vol. 1038–9. For a discussion of the methodology employed, see appendix II.

III

The establishment of the Banque du Peuple did not satisfy the need for credit facilities on the part of francophone merchants. This was made abundantly clear by the men who gained a charter to establish the Banque des Marchands in 1846. As Tulchinsky has noted, 'A very large segment, perhaps a majority, of [Montreal's] French Canadian merchants, including many with impeccable credit ratings, supported the bank because "il est notoire qu'il devient de jour en jour plus difficile d'avoir l'aide des institutions financiers de cette ville, même avec le meilleur papier."'[21] But like many banks which received charters from the legislature, the Banque des Marchands failed to gain the capital needed to begin operations and disappeared from view without a trace.

More successful, however, were four other francophone banks that began operations in Quebec's two largest cities between 1860 and 1874. The first of these to open its doors was the Banque Nationale, the only French bank to be situated in Quebec City. The Nationale was largely the product of the determination of the leaders of the Caisse d'Economie de Notre-Dame de Québec to establish a francophone chartered bank in the old capital. The Caisse d'Economie was a savings bank established in 1848 by certain members of Quebec City's elite, allegedly to encourage thrift among the workers. It was barred by provincial statute from accepting deposits of more than £500 from any individual and could only invest its funds in public securities or the stock of chartered banks. Accordingly, the Caisse d'Economie and its sister institution, the Montreal-based City and District Savings Bank, were the largest holders of bank stock in Canada in 1881.[22] The savings banks were also barred from making collateral loans until 1866, and even then such loans could only be made upon the sort of securities noted above. In Quebec City, where the Quebec Bank was the only game in town in the 1850s, the Caisse d'Economie could not satisfy the needs of the local francophone merchants, which led some of its leaders to the idea of forming a chartered bank.

From 1849 to 1870 the physician Olivier Robitaille was the

president of the savings bank, and it was his leadership that linked the Caisse d'Economie to the Banque Nationale project. He had been part of a delegation that had tried to gain a branch of the Banque du Peuple for Quebec City, but when that effort failed he turned his sights to the idea of a chartered bank. Robitaille convinced his fellow directors of the savings bank to include a reference in its 1856 report regarding the need 'à fonder à Québec une banque pour faciliter le commerce local, et par là venir en aide aux industriels qui n'ont pas toujours des capitaux en mains pour donner l'élan nécessaire à leurs affaires.'[23] That this was to be a French institution was clear to Robitaille from the start. In the 1870s he noted, 'J'avais toujours pensé que cette banque devrait être purement canadienne[-française], et ne pas y voir l'élément anglais dans sa formation.'[24]

By July 1858 Robitaille believed that the time had finally arrived to launch the project in an active manner. Because only a small capital was to be employed at the start, 'il semblait qu'il serait facile de le trouver parmi nos marchands, nos industriels et les petits rentiers.' Accordingly, he prepared a list of 'soixante noms canadiens pris dans les différentes classes de la société,' and called them together for a meeting at the Caisse d'Economie. All expressed enthusiasm for the project, which stood to aid their businesses, and they urged Robitaille to petition the government for a charter. It was received in 1859 and required the collection of $250,000 in capital in one year, lest the charter be lost. Robitaille soon found that it was easier to receive verbal support for his project than it was to secure the capital investment of merchants whose means were often limited. He later admitted that he felt foolish for having chosen to preclude English investment, and it was only the last-minute heroics of another one of the founders, Ulric Tessier, who found twenty francophones willing to subscribe $8,000 each, that saved the bank from losing its charter.[25]

The bank opened for business in 1860 with a capital almost entirely subscribed by francophones and with an entirely French board of directors. Most of the directors were merchants and all of them could also be found on the board of the Caisse d'Economie. Typical was the hardware merchant Eugène Chinic, who was the bank's initial vice-president and who became its president in the 1870s. However, Robitaille's dream of a purely French institution was unrealistic if the bank hoped to expand. In its first fifteen years of operations the Banque Nationale showed itself to be very different from the Banque du Peuple as its authorized capital of $1 million was paid up by 1866 and a further $1 million was added to its authorized limit in 1872. The Nationale's lack of conservatism was also evident in its opening two branches in 1872, in its doubling its assets between 1871 and 1874, and in its paying out dividends that tended to be higher than those paid by comparable Quebec banks even though its profits ran below the norm.[26] This last practice had only been possible by failing to write off bad debts, which remained on the Nationale's books and which were to create headaches when the boom years of the early 1870s were replaced by the depression of the later years of the decade.

The bank's expansionist policy made it the largest francophone bank by 1874, but in the process important English investors came to the Nationale. By 1873 nearly 30% of the bank's stock was in the hands of English interests, and in return for their money anglophones gained seats on the board of directors and became important clients. It must be remembered that English-speaking merchants in Quebec City also had no alternative to the Quebec Bank in the early 1860s, and when Robitaille's visions of linguistic purity were dropped English investors quickly emerged. In 1861 Abraham Joseph took a seat on the board, a position that he held until 1874 when he left to help establish the Stadacona Bank in Quebec City. Joseph, a Jew, was an outsider just as DeWitt had been in Montreal and was a likely ally for the French merchants. When Joseph departed, his place on the board was taken by Henry Atkinson because of the latter's 'connections with the lumber and timber trade.'[27] This connection with English-speaking lumber merchants dated back to as early as 1863 when substantial credit was extended to leading figures of the local trade such as D.C. Thomson and James Gibb, both of whom later went on to aid in the establishment of the Union Bank in the city. It would even appear that the establishment of the bank's second branch at Ottawa was designed to serve these lumber interests.

The Banque Nationale had been conceived as an institution which would have 'une physionomie purement canadienne-française,' but the reality of the capital market changed the operations of the bank as it sought to expand.[28] The same scenario also held true for the Banque Jacques-Cartier, which was formed by a group of francophone merchants in Montreal in 1861 and which opened its doors early in 1862 with an authorized capital of $1 million. The bank was led by the dry-goods merchant Jean-Louis Beaudry from 1861 to 1869 and by the pharmacist and merchant Romuald Trudeau from 1869 to 1875. Their goal was to 'serve the French Canadian trade,' and they were joined in the early years of the bank's existence by other francophone investors so that 90% of the Jacques-Cartier's capital of $850,000 was held by French speakers in 1865.[29]

In the decade that followed, the bank energetically expanded its operations, rapidly seeking out savings deposits and working to expand its note circulation in a manner similar to that evident in the affairs of the Banque Nationale, but very different from the Banque du Peuple. In fact, the Jacques-Cartier was the largest French bank in terms of assets for a short period in the early 1870s. So rapid was the bank's growth that one French journal commented in 1870, 'La Banque Jacques-Cartier grâce à son admirable gestion est aujourd'hui à la tête des institutions financières canadiennes-françaises de Montréal et rivalise sur le marché avec les institutions anglaises de premier ordre.'[30] But there was a price to be paid for what the bank referred to as a policy of 'satisfying all legitimate demands [for credit].'[31] The bank did a large business, but not always a highly profitable one. While its profits as a percentage of paid capital ran slightly below the average for other Quebec banks of its size in the 1860s, the gap widened during the early 1870s. By 1873 the Jacques-Cartier's figure was less than 10% while comparable Quebec banks were earning 14% upon their capital. At the same time the bank managed to build up a substantial reserve fund and to pay dividends that were generally higher than those paid by banks of a similar size. Like the Nationale, the Jacques-Cartier was failing to write bad debts off its books, a policy that was to plague it in the late 1870s.

The bank's aggressive policy also forced it to look beyond the French community for sources of capital. Between 1865 and 1875 its capital increased by slightly more than $1 million, nearly 30% of which came from English-speaking investors. This change in the character of the Jacques-Cartier's shareholders brought the first English-speaking director, the importer J.L. Cassidy, to its board in 1871, and led to its involvement in projects as far removed from Quebec as the financing of a railway in Prince Edward Island. The emergence of minor English banks in Montreal such as the Exchange Bank, the Mechanics Bank, and the Metropolitan Bank during this decade had apparently not satisfied the desire on the part of marginal members of the city's English business community to gain a foothold in the world of finance. With French sources of financing strictly limited, the expansion of the Jacques-Cartier provided an opening for these English investors.

Such English investment was less visible in the establishment of two more French banks in Montreal near the end of this period, but this was only due to the fact that the capital investment in each was still minimal in 1875. The first of the two, the Banque Ville-Marie, began business in 1872 with a board of directors dominated by francophone merchants. Its paid capital in 1875 was less than $650,000, and by 1880 it had still not reached its authorized limit of $1 million. Because of its limited need for capital, 90% of the Ville-Marie's stock was still in the hands of francophones at the start of the 1880s. Similarly, the Banque d'Hochelaga was incorporated in 1873 as a result of the petitioning of the government by twelve men, all of whom identified themselves as 'traders.'[32] The Hochelaga, which was to become the most successful of the French banks, began business in 1874 with a paid capital of less than $400,000, a figure which barely increased during the late 1870s owing to the impact of the depressed economic times. Accordingly, in 1881 the bank's capital was still only $680,000 a far cry from its authorized limit of $1 million, and nearly 90% of this amount was provided by francophones.

By 1875 there were four French banks operating in Montreal with another based in Quebec City. There might have been a fifth bank in Montreal had the promoters of the Banque St-Jean Baptiste, who received their charter in 1875, been able to find the needed capital. This failure is not entirely surprising when one looks at the background of the promoters of the St-Jean Baptiste. While the banks that got off the ground were promoted by businessmen, particularly merchants, this project had men behind it who were evenly divided between those in various lines of business and those in the liberal professions. One of the promoters, Louis-Etienne Avila Valois, was even a priest.[33] It was hard enough for the other banks to start up with the backing of businessmen who might bring their business to the new banks. Even in these cases expansion was only possible by gaining access to English investment capital. It was futile for francophones in an even weaker business position to believe that they could start up a bank.

I V

The final two French banks to have been established by 1874 operated in an entirely different environment from those which were formed in Quebec's two major centres. While the French merchants of Montreal and Quebec City might have felt deprived of sufficient accommodation from the English banks, at least there were banks present from which certain services could be received by all. For instance, it was through the banks that a supply of paper money was made available. In the smaller centres of the province, however, even the existence of a circulating medium could not be taken for granted in the total absence of banking facilities. For precisely this reason a leading Sherbrooke businessman wrote to an official of the Bank of Montreal in 1836, seeking the establishment of a branch in the Eastern Townships, but to no avail.[34] When banking facilities were still not available in the area in 1854, a group of businessmen sought to create a bank of their own. Their petition noted that they 'suffer great inconvenience from the want of a local bank through which to transact their business. The commercial, mechanical and agricultural interests of the Townships are retarded and enterprise checked by the deprivation of that accommodation ... The managing class of those [Montreal] institutions have little or no interest in our part of the province.'[35] The Eastern Townships Bank received its charter in 1855 and opened for business in 1859, and, as one might expect from a region whose population was overwhelmingly English, all of the bank's directors, most of its clients, and nearly all of its shareholders were English.[36]

Circumstances similar to those faced by the Townships in the 1850s led to the establishment of two other chartered banks on the plain to the southeast of Montreal during the early 1870s. This region had no banking facilities as late as 1871 to serve its almost 250,000 people. Accordingly, it is not surprising that movements to establish locally operated banks began in two of the larger centres of the region, and since the populations of both St-Jean and St-Hyacinthe were overwhelmingly French these two towns gave rise to institutions that were French in almost every regard.

Because of its location just to the north of some major rapids which obstructed traffic along the Lake Champlain–Richelieu River route, St-Jean was an important centre in the middle of the nineteenth century. Its role as a trans-shipment point for goods moving between Montreal and New England made it larger than other nearby service centres such as St-Hyacinthe or Sherbrooke by 1851. But the construction of the St Lawrence and Atlantic Railway through the last two cities meant the end of St-Jean's locational advantages, and by 1871 its population had fallen well behind that of its competitors. During the last third of the nineteenth century the leaders of St-Jean devised a number of strategies to try to revive the town's fortunes. The most costly of these efforts was the granting of over $200,000 in loans and bonuses by the city in order to attract manufacturing to the town, but to no avail.[37]

It was under these rather depressing economic prospects that the Banque de St-Jean received its charter in 1873. The largely French-speaking group of men who petitioned for this charter were not primarily businessmen as had been the case with the other French banks that started up elsewhere, and this may well say something about the assessment by local merchants of the

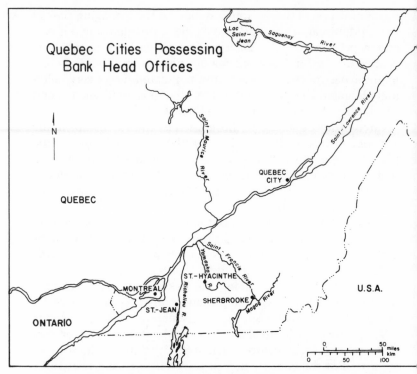

Quebec Cities Possessing Bank Head Offices

likelihood that a bank in St-Jean could really operate successfully. The moving force behind the securing of the charter and the bank's first president was Louis Molleur, a local businessman and member of the Legislative Assembly. As for the rest of the petitioners, they were primarily notaries and lawyers.

The viability of the Banque de St-Jean was also in question at the start because of issues regarding its shareholders. In order to begin operations a bank was required to have $500,000 of its capital subscribed and $100,000 of this amount had to be paid up; it was normal for the federal Treasury Board to look over the list of proposed shareholders before giving a bank permission to open its doors. The Banque de St-Jean first attempted to secure this approval by submitting a list of shareholders in July 1873. This list contained only nine shareholders, who collectively had sub-scribed for $540,000 of bank stock, $479,000 of which was to be acquired by the Société Permanente de Construction du District d'Iberville.[38] One wonders how a building society whose own paid capital was only $127,000 and whose total assets amounted to less than $250,000 was in any position to make such an invest-ment, but the financial capacity of this organization was probably less important than the fact that seven of the nine promoters of the Banque de St-Jean, including Molleur, were also directors of the building society. In any event, the Treasury Board took a dim view of nearly 90% of a bank's stock being held by one corporate shareholder, and it rejected the list.

The bank's promoters came back with a second list that did not include the building society; but while the number of prospective shareholders increased from nine to fifty-seven, much of the slack was taken up by Molleur and his friends from the building society's board of directors, who increased their investment from the $58,000 noted on the first list to nearly $250,000. In regard to the second list, the Treasury Board found new causes for concern. As one official noted, 'If the list now sent had come originally, I have no doubt it would have been accepted at once as it has not, on former occasions, been customary to make any investigations into the standing of the names included in the list. But as the original proposition had been of so unsound a character, I re-quested the Assistant Receiver General to cause enquiries to be made as to the means of the provisional shareholders.' The report indicated that $328,000 worth of shares on the new list had been taken on by people of good economic standing, while the remain-ing $185,400, or 36% of the total, was to go to individuals whose affairs were described as either 'doubtful' or "bad.'[39]

The government wanted to be certain that the investors in a new bank had the means to pay their double liability to the creditors should the bank fail. One would think that the second list of Banque de St-Jean shareholders would have failed this test, but a certificate to begin operations was granted in spite of the shareholders' limitations. Equally curious was the government's lack of concern over whether $100,000 of the bank's capital had been paid in specie, as required by law, before it opened for business. As one of the shareholders later noted, 'the greater part [of the $100,000] was paid with the product of notes which the subscribers and promoters of the said bank discounted.'[40]

The cloud that seemed to hang over the Banque de St-Jean from its inception did not dissipate once it began operations in October 1873. On its first anniversary the following anonymous letter appeared in the *Monetary Times*: 'I beg to call your attention to the returns of the Banque de St-Jean furnished the Public Auditor for the month ending June [1874]. As they [i.e. the bank] had then only been in existence for a little over nine months and had gratified or satisfied their shareholders by paying two dividends at the rate of eight per cent per annum, and had not as yet honored the public with their annual report, I think you will allow it is time that their affairs should bear the "light."' The correspondent went on to note that the bank's loans amounted to $232,000, most of which 'had been lent to the Directors to aid in the paying up of their stocks, and for speculations in real estate in Montreal.'[41] Nor did the bank escape complaints in later years regarding the secrecy with which it operated. It never published its annual report with any regularity, and even appears to have kept no minutes of directors' meetings, so no records of decisions could be found.[42]

The establishment of the Banque de St-Jean was largely the product of a few local opportunists who sought a bank charter to serve their own limited interests. This is not to say that the other French banks were conceived out of any charitable desire to provide service to the public at large. In most cases they emerged to facilitate the dealings of francophone merchants, but at least in those cases there was legitimate business being supported by banks of some means. In the case of the Banque de St-Jean, there was relatively little evidence of any interest by local merchants to promote the bank, which commenced operations with a paid capital that was less than that required by law.

Only twenty-five miles away, at St-Hyacinthe, a very different bank was being formed at the same time that the Banque de

St-Jean was coming into existence. While St-Jean's economic prospects had been damaged by the construction of the St Lawrence and Atlantic Railway, St-Hyacinthe's economic future was enhanced when the railway arrived in 1848. In the 1840s St-Hyacinthe emerged as a market town of some importance for the agricultural products of the region, but the difficulties of sending goods out from the city either by road or by the Yamaska River, upon which St-Hyacinthe was located, hindered its growth. The roads tended to be impassable during parts of the year, while the rapids in the Yamaska, which provided a potential source of power for industry, blocked navigation. In this context, the railway was greeted with enthusiasm by local businessmen, but they soon found that a railway alone could not change the town's economic fortunes. The population of St-Hyacinthe increased by only 13% between 1851 and 1871, and by the latter date only three of the town's industries were employing more than ten workers. Even agricultural production in the region increased by only 8% during the 1850s and 1860s as opposed to 59% for the province as a whole.[43]

Businessmen and farmers alike began to blame the absence of financial institutions as the key to the region's problems when the railway did not turn out to be the area's panacea. As early as the mid-1850s, farmers from the region were calling for the establishment of a bank that would serve their particular needs.[44] In the 1860s the Banque Agricole movement, a forerunner of the drive to establish caisses populaires across rural Quebec, took on greater substance under the leadership of George de Boucherville from St-Hyacinthe. Ultimately, this effort floundered because of 'l'influence des autres banques et de la part des capitalistes.'[45] Similarly fruitless were the efforts by merchants and manufacturers from the city to gain a branch bank for St-Hyacinthe. As early as 1861 *Le Courrier de St-Hyacinthe* was resigned to the city's banklessness: 'Disons que vouloir inviter les banques de Montréal à ouvrir des banques succursales en cette ville est chose inutile.'[46] But while this newspaper may have been resigned to the futility of trying to gain a branch bank for St-Hyacinthe, it continued to point out the difficulties for the town in the absence of facilities 'si nécessaires au développement du commerce et de l'industrie de notre ville.'[47]

If neither an unorthodox institution such as the Banque Agricole nor a branch of one of the existing banks was likely to appear in the region, then the answer was for residents of the area to form their own chartered bank. The idea of establishing just such a bank with its head office at St-Hyacinthe had circulated in the local press since at least 1857, but the notion only gained an important following during the economic expansion of the early 1870s which saw the opening of seventeen new banks in Canada between 1871 and 1873.[48] A public assembly held early in 1871 to launch the drive to incorporate the Banque de St-Hyacinthe seems to have accomplished nothing more than to have brought the town its first bank branch. The Merchants' Bank, fearful that a market might be lost, opened the long-desired branch only weeks after the assembly. The presence of this branch made some of the supporters of the Banque de St-Hyacinthe sceptical about whether the project could really succeed, and these people chose in 1872 to establish a financial institution with a more limited mandate by forming the Société Permanente de Construction d'Yamaska.[49]

The idea of creating this local bank was not dead, for a group of ten men finally received a charter for the Banque de St-Hyacinthe in 1873. Nine of the petitioners were French, eight were businessmen, and seven were from St-Hyacinthe. St-Hyacinthe businessmen such as Georges-Casimir Dessaulles, whose Compagnie Manufacturière de St-Hyacinthe stood to gain credit from such a bank, and Romuald St-Jacques, whose private banking firm was to form the basis of the new bank's affairs, had too much to gain to let the project drop. Once they received the charter they went throughout the region to market the bank's $500,000 in capital, all of which was subscribed within four months. Unlike the situation surrounding the establishment of the Banque de St-Jean, this bank was able to sell its stock to nearly five hundred people, the majority of whom lived outside the city and 40% of whom were farmers. Still, there should be no doubt that this was an institution firmly under the control of St-Hyacinthe businessmen, who dominated the first board of directors. Their dominance was achieved through their control of large blocks of bank stock. As Laurent Lapointe has indicated, Dessaulles and those clearly associated with him owned over one-quarter of total bank stock, making them an unequal match for the numerous farmers who owned only a few shares each.[50] When the ledgers of R. St-Jacques et Compagnie were taken over by the Banque de St-Hyacinthe in January 1874, a new bank opened whose operations – like those of all the French banks except the Banque de St-Jean – started out firmly under the control of francophone businessmen.

Although the banks established at St-Jean and St-Hyacinthe were different from one another in almost every respect, they were united by the fact that they were the only French banks to be established outside the province's two major centres. But in addition to these two instances in which banks were formed, there was also the case of Trois-Rivières, where efforts to establish a bank repeatedly failed. The first attempt came in 1841 when Moses Hart and other Trois-Rivières merchants petitioned the government for a bank charter, apparently to no avail since there is no further trace of this effort.[51] A second attempt, but the first led by the city's French population, came in 1857 with the issuing of a prospectus for the establishment of the Banque des Trois-Rivières, whose capital was to be set at $100,000. Residents of the region were called upon to support 'une institution monétaire qui tout en offrant d'immenses avantages au commerce, à l'agriculture, et à l'industrie offrirait également aux Capitalistes et aux actionnaires un placement certain.'[52] But once more no charter was secured. Marginally more successful was the 1873 effort by local interests, most of whom were French, which did secure a charter for a Banque des Trois-Rivières, but which did not result in the opening of a new bank since the needed capital could not be found.[53]

The failed attempts of both 1857 and 1873 were directly related to the fact that Trois-Rivières was not a bankless town in either year. By the time of the 1857 drive, branches of the Quebec Bank and the Bank of Montreal had already been established; the local press could complain about the nature, but not the existence, of local banking facilities. *L'Ere Nouvelle* noted in 1857, 'Il est vrai que depuis quelques années des agences de différentes banques ont été établies en cette ville, mais au lieu de favoriser le commerce, l'industrie et l'agriculture, nous pouvons dire qu'elles ont été au contraire un moyen de les gêner dans leurs opérations, car la plupart de ces agences de Banque ne sont destinées qu'à reçevoir les dépots ...'[54] By 1873 the Bank of Montreal had departed, but its place was taken by the Union Bank. As for the Quebec Bank, it could hardly be accused of draining funds from Trois-Rivières where its loans were exceeding deposits by over $200,000.[55]

With some banking facilities present, it was impossible for the local press to mobilize people to risk their capital on the Banque des Trois-Rivières. In St-Hyacinthe *Le Courrier* might argue that supporting the local bank was 'non seulement un plaisir mais aussi un devoir,' but in Trois-Rivières this would have made no sense.[56] *Le Journal des Trois-Rivières* was confident that the 1873 effort would succeed because of the availability of capital which was evident from the investment by local residents of $60,000 in Montreal and Quebec City banks during a six-month period in 1872.[57] Indeed, by 1881 this investment had reached $275,000; but as long as other banks were present none of this was going to go to a Banque des Trois-Rivières. In particular, the town's francophone business leaders stayed away in both 1857 and 1873. Doctors, lawyers, and notaries led the way in the drive for a bank at Trois-Rivières, but as has already been seen local businessmen were essential for the establishment of a bank.

v

At the start of 1875 the seven French banks had total assets of nearly $18 million. Whether or not this was a substantial amount depends entirely upon one's perspective. When considered in the light of a historiography that has often ignored the existence of francophone enterprise during this period, this sum might appear significant. These banks were led, to a great degree financed, and overwhelmingly patronized by francophones. That there was sufficient business activity to call these banks into existence was indicative of changes that were gradually taking place in Quebec agriculture and of the growth of industry in the province. This activity had given rise to successful merchants such as Pierre Jodoin of the Banque du Peuple and Eugène Chinic of the Banque Nationale who now sought banks to support their commercial ventures. They belonged to what Paul-André Linteau has described as Quebec's 'moyenne bourgeoisie.' The men within this group generally operated firms whose activities were of some significance within the Quebec economy but which did not generally extend beyond the province. As Linteau has noted, 'A cause de l'ampleur plus restreinte de ses moyens, ses interventions se font généralement dans un contexte régional.'[58] These businessmen bore little resemblance to the francophone elites of mid-century described by Fernand Ouellet as still possessing 'mentalités d'Ancien Régime.'[59]

In a different perspective the $18-million figure appears far less impressive, for it amounted to less than 10% of the total assets of Canada's banks. Moreover, it must be remembered that even this scale of operations had only been achieved through the support of English clients. All three of the French banks which functioned for some time prior to 1875 required significant amounts of English capital, and in the one case in which branches were established the Banque Nationale seems to have located them to serve English lumber interests. The assets and the liabilities of the French institutions as a group did not differ greatly from the English banks of Quebec of a similar size, but there was as yet no indication that French bank operations could be supported by a broad francophone clientele.[60] Without this support the French banks stood to face the same oblivion awaiting the smaller English banks across Canada whose clientele was lost when the larger institutions came to expand their operations.

By 1875 a group of francophone businessmen had indicated its ability to bring a number of banks into existence. This had been achieved in the context of the spectacular expansion of competition within the Canadian banking industry, paticularly in the early 1870s, and because of the increased economic activity within Quebec that had made banking an attractive pursuit for a number of French speaking entrepreneurs. But what had still not been made clear by 1875 was whether there was a market capable of supporting these institutions over the long run.

3

Hard Times: 1875–1900

The number of chartered banks in operation in Canada fell from an all-time high of fifty-one in 1875 to thirty-five at the start of the new century. The banks that passed from the scene were generally smaller institutions that were particularly vulnerable to the impact of repeated downturns in the economy and to mismanagement by their administrators. At the same time that some of the smaller banks were closing shop, the larger ones were greatly expanding their operations with the result that the total assets of all of Canada's banks more than doubled during this period.

Nowhere were these changes clearer than in Quebec's two leading banking centres, Montreal and Quebec City.[1] At the start of 1875, sixteen banks had headquarters in the two cities, but only eight of these still existed at the close of 1900. The ranks of the English banks were depleted by the passing of the Metropolitan, Mechanics, Exchange, and City banks in Montreal, and the Stadacona Bank in Quebec City. Their disappearance was more than made up for, however, by the expansion of English institutions such as the Bank of Montreal and the Merchants' Bank. As for the French banks, the Banque du Peuple and the Banque Ville-Marie failed in the late 1890s, while the Banque Jacques-Cartier was forced to change its name in 1900 as part of a reorganization designed to save the bank from liquidation. The Banque

Nationale limped through most of this period before righting itself in the late 1890s, and only the Banque d'Hochelaga steadily expanded its assets between 1875 and 1900. The result was that the assets of the French banks, which had amounted to nearly $18 million at the start of 1875, totalled only $20 million by 1900. During the same period the percentage of total Canadian bank assets controlled by the French banks fell from 10% to 5%.

While the French banks had their problems during this period, they also had at least one major success by demonstrating that they could finance their operations through mobilizing the savings of francophone Quebecers. The modernization of Quebec agriculture, particularly in the plain to the southeast of Montreal, together with the province's increasing industrialization, left some people with savings that they could deposit in one of the numerous branches established by the French banks or which they could invest in the capital stock of these institutions. These savings were all too often lost because of the poor management of several of the banks. Nevertheless, it had been shown that francophone Quebecers possessed a significant pool of savings upon which banking operations could be built.

I I

It is unlikely that many observers of the Montreal business scene in the 1870s would have guessed that the Banque du Peuple would be the first French bank to go out of business. By 1875 the bank had generated a good deal of confidence among the population through its conservative and stable management, and there was little evidence in its annual reports during the decade leading up to its fiftieth anniversary in 1885 to shake that confidence. C.S. Cherrier, an *associé gérant* of the bank since 1865, served as president throughout most of the decade, while A.A. Trottier was cashier throughout the period. The bank seemed to handle the depression years of the 1870s reasonably well. It was forced to liquidate its reserve fund and to reduce its dividends from 8% in 1875 to 4% in 1880. Still, dividends were being paid which were generally higher than those issued by other banks of the same size, and the Banque du Peuple was spared the suspensions of business and rumours of merger that hounded the other French banks. Some shareholders began to wonder why their dividends did not rise above the 5% level with the lifting of the depression in the early 1880s, but they received little response from the directors, who were not obliged by the bank's charter to provide such explanations.

The veil of secrecy shrouding the Banque du Peuple's affairs was lifted partially in 1880 when the bank made its net profits for the year public for the first time. These figures indicated that, because of low profits, the bank was incapable of either paying a higher dividend or of re-establishing its reserve fund. Throughout the first half of the 1880s, the bank's net profits as a percentage of its paid capital never exceeded 5.2%, while the figure for other Quebec banks of its size never fell below 6.8%. In 1883 the gap was at its widest, as Banque du Peuple profits stood at 5% of paid capital while the percentage for comparable banks was nearly 10%. In paying its 5% dividend in that year the bank left nothing for writing off bad debts or building up the reserve.

The bank earned relatively low profits as it continued to follow business practices that may have made sense in the 1850s or 1860s, but which were no longer relevant in the 1880s. In 1888 J.S. Bousquet, who was Trottier's successor as cashier, made the following diagnosis of the Banque du Peuple's affairs: 'La fondation des nouvelles banques, la politique adoptée par toutes les autres banques d'agrandissement de leurs opérations par l'établissement de succursales ... a créé une compétition très grande, diminué le taux d'intérêt et intercepté les dépôts de la campagne qui autrefois trouvaient leur chemin jusqu'à nous; notre cercle d'opérations devient d'année en année plus restreint; aussi en comparant nos états de 1875 avec 1885, nous constatons durant ces 10 années une diminution progressive de nos dépôts et de notre circulation, et nos prêts et escomptes au commerce étaient $500,000 plus élevés en 1875. La conséquence a été que les profits nets réalisés diminuèrent, et nous étions arrivés à une période où il était difficile pour cette institution de faire un commerce avantageux avec ses ressources.'[2] To make matters worse, Bousquet found that the directors, 'toujours engagés dans la même routine,' were extending credit upon securities which were of little, if any, immediately realizable value.

By the mid-1800s, the Banque du Peuple neeaed to make a drastic change in the way in which it operated if it hoped to become profitable once again. Accordingly, in 1885 the directors suspended dividend payments for the first time in the bank's history and asked the shareholders to reduce the value of their investment by 25%. The bank's capital would then be set at $1.2 million, with $400,000 being set free for the establishment of a reserve fund and the purging of bad debts from the books. This request indicated that the normally conservative directors were capable of some imagination when their wealth was on the line. After all, if the bank had been forced to liquidate its affairs, it was the directors that would have been held personally liable for any outstanding demands on the part of creditors. By securing a reduction in the value of the shareholders' investment, the directors stood to transfer some of the burden from their own shoulders. With barely a word of protest, the shareholders obliged the directors and agreed to the reduction.

The directors had only begun to change the face of the Banque du Peuple. The first hint of further changes came at the bank's 1885 annual meeting when the long-timer director, Jacques Grenier, remarked that 'c'était l'intention des directeurs d'ouvrir des succursales et augmenter ainsi la circulation.'[3] Within two months Grenier would be the new president of the bank, and in 1887 the change in leadership was completed with Bousquet's appointment as cashier. The Grenier-Bousquet team pushed for the rapid expansion of the bank's affairs, and under their leadership assets, which had increased by only 45% between 1857 and 1885, grew by 190% in the decade that followed. This expansion was not financed out of an increase of the bank's capital. Rather, funds were raised through the growth of the note circulation by 170% and, more important, the increase of total deposits by over 400%. The key to this strategy was the establishment of branches, the first of which was opened in 1885 on the fiftieth anniversary of the bank. By 1895 there were ten branches aiding in the amassing of savings deposits of over $5 million. So heavily did the bank lean upon deposits that the percentage of its liabilities owed to depositors was the highest of any Canadian bank at the start of 1895.

Throughout this decade of expansion the majority of Banque du Peuple shares continued to rest in the hands of English-speaking interests. Investors such as Senator Donald Macmillan retained a stake in the bank because they believed that 'the directors were responsible to the last dollar they were worth.'[4] In spite of this English investment, the bank was, because of its unique organization, entirely under the control of its directors, most of whom were French-speaking businessmen. It was under their influence that all but one of the branches were established in towns over 75% of whose population was French, thus bringing the bank a primarily French-speaking clientele. As Bousquet noted in 1888, 'Nos avances sont faites principalement au commerce canadien-français de cette province, et à son progrès, l'avenir de cette institution est intéressé, car nous en avons une grande partie.'[5] In only one case did the Banque du Peuple try to set up shop in a town with a significant English population, but the experience in Coaticook, whose population was evenly divided between French and English speakers, was so bad that the branch was closed after only two years. The problems for a French bank in penetrating the English market were also to be experienced by other institutions.

With its rapid expansion and its emphasis upon serving a French clientele, the Banque du Peuple and its leading lights, Grenier and Bousquet, became the favourites of the French press during the late 1880s and early 1890s. In 1887 *Le Moniteur du Commerce* praised Grenier for giving the bank 'une sécurité et une respectabilité qui lui permettent de rivaliser avec n'importe quelle banque anglaise.'[6] In 1890 *Le Prix Courant* speculated that 'si la banque eût été dès le commencement sous la direction énergique et active du bureau actuel, elle tiendrait aujourd'hui un des premiers rangs parmi les banques du Canada.'[7] *La Revue Canadienne* added its voice by praising the bank upon the opening of its new head office building in 1894. '[Sa] prospérité et le mouvement d'affaires toujours croissant qui y correspond ont rendu indispensable la construction du nouvel édifice, qui est un des plus beaux ornements de notre ville.'[8]

Within a year of the opening of its handsome new headquarters, the Banque du Peuple closed its doors, never to open them again. In the light of the praise that had been heaped upon it, the Banque du Peuple's suspension on 16 July 1895 came as a surprise to most observers. As the *Monetary Times* noted, 'The French residents of Quebec from the habitant to the curé regarded La Banque du Peuple much as the English people regard the Bank of Montreal. It was the oldest French bank; its bills were familiar, and ... the popular belief in it was strong.'[9]

The first hints that there was something wrong came in early July when Bousquet resigned as cashier, only four months after tabling another rosy picture of the bank's fortunes. The first reports regarding Bousquet's departure referred to an honest difference of opinion regarding administrative practices, but soon it became public knowledge that the disagreement was over Bousquet's granting of nearly $1.5 million of credit without the approval of the directors and with little security from the borrowers. By the end of the year Bousquet had fled to the United States to avoid prosecution, but in the short term his departure provoked a run on the bank by its depositors who were fearful for their money. In all, $2 million was withdrawn between 30 June and 31 July 1895. The Bank of Montreal and other banks came to the rescue with $1 million in aid to pay off the depositors and to halt the run, but it was to no avail as the Banque du Peuple was forced to suspend operations.[10]

The surprise which resulted from the suspension was no doubt linked to the fact that the bank had earned profits generally greater than those of comparable Quebec banks throughout most of the decade prior to 1895. Its image of responsible business behaviour was aided by the paying of dividends below the norm with the remaining funds going to building up a substantial reserve fund. However, in spite of this veneer of respectability there was a fatal flaw in the bank's affairs.

As has already been seen, the bank was highly dependent

upon savings deposits to finance its operations. In theory, these savings were distinguishable from deposits left in current accounts: the former could only be withdrawn upon the depositor's giving of notice, usually ten to fifteen days, while funds in current accounts could be withdrawn upon demand. In practice, however, there was little distinction between the two forms of deposits. In his 1909 *Manual of Canadian Banking*, H.M.P. Eckhardt noted that there was only a 'thin line between current and savings accounts,' as the fifteen days' notice was rarely exacted.[11] Given this situation, the leaders of the Banque du Peuple were in no position to halt the withdrawal of $1.4 million of savings deposits during July 1895. Had they taken the unusual step of exercising their right to delay payment, the already shaky confidence in the bank would have been further compromised, and to repay the depositors would have required the discovery of funds that were not readily available. Accordingly, the Banque du Peuple was the first of the French banks to discover the implications of dependence upon savings deposits the hard way.

Because of the changed structure of its liabilities, away from shareholders' funds and towards a reliance upon savings deposits, the bank needed to invest its assets in a way that might readily yield funds. In fact, however, only a small portion of its assets was invested in call loans secured by stocks and bonds or was held in the form of specie. Such assets would have earned relatively little for the bank, but at least they would have provided a means of holding off unhappy depositors. Instead, the Banque du Peuple placed the bulk of its assets, 80% at the time of its suspension, into the wide array of loans and discounts included under the title of 'current loans.' This 80% figure was well above that for Quebec banks in general and was also higher than the figure for banks of a comparable size. In the best of times these loans could earn the bank handsome profits, and as long as the savings continued to pour in, even if some of the loans turned sour, the volume of business might permit profitable affairs. However, the problem was what to do when a large number of depositors wanted their savings back at the same time since these loans could not be immediately recovered from the borrowers. By

1895 Bousquet had lent out $1.5 million upon little security, and even before his indiscretions the Department of Finance was aware of other bad debts of nearly $500,000 being carried on the bank's books. Funds sufficient to pay back the depositors could not readily be found, and a suspension of operations was the only option.

Because of the Banque du Peuple's reliance upon savings deposits, its suspension ushered in the beginning of a long battle between the depositors and the directors regarding the repayment of these funds. From the directors' point of view, what was essential was to avoid the attachment of their personal wealth to pay back the creditors as was called for by the bank's charter. The first of a series of manoeuvres designed to prevent this from happening came in October 1895 when the directors asked the depositors to accept repayment of their funds over the course of two years. The bank's leaders indicated that this commitment was required so as to resume normal operations prior to the ninetieth day following the suspension. The Bank Act stipulated that no resumption could take place after ninety days, but in spite of the depositors' commitment to the directors, the reopening never occurred, nor is it likely that it was ever really planned.[12]

Between October 1895 and October 1897 the depositors were supposed to be repaid at six-month intervals, and in fact the first two instalments of 25% each were paid. But by early 1897 the directors were seeking a further two years to complete repayment. The depositors could have gone to court to demand that the wealth of the directors be seized so that immediate repayment might take place. However, legal action was not a serious option for the francophone depositors of limited means. Accordingly, they fell in line at a meeting held in March 1897, which was described in rather sad terms by one observer: 'I saw poor old women with tears in their eyes in shabby thin frocks and only a match on their head; their savings and the savings of others had been squandered, sunk in a cesspool of fraud and immorality.'[13] Fearful that the depositors might still go to the courts to gain repayment before 1899, the directors went to Ottawa to seek special legislation forbidding such actions. This bill was described by a correspondent to Charles Tupper as an effort by the directors 'to pay no amount if possible,' but it became law just the same.[14]

By the fall of 1898 a further payment of only 5% had been made to the depositors and the directors were seeking another extension, this time to 1901. When the depositors demanded an immediate repayment of $200,000 in exchange for the extension, the directors balked.[15] However, they came back with a counter-offer in early 1899 by which they would make a final payment of 20% within two years, bringing the total paid to 75%. This 20% was to come out of the disposal of the Bank's remaining assets. If the assets could yield more than the roughly $680,000 needed to be done with the depositors, the directors would get the rest; if the assets could not provide the $680,000, the directors would make up the difference out of their pockets, up to a maximum of $200,000.

For only $200,000 the directors stood to free themselves from the responsibility of repaying the $1.5 million in deposits still outstanding; and on the odd chance that the assets, whose book value was still $1.5 million, could yield more than $680,000, the directors stood to walk away with more money in their pockets. The beleaguered depositors accepted the deal, but eyebrows were raised in Ottawa when the directors again sought parliamentary approval to protect themselves from any legal action. Israël Tarte was not alone when he advised finance minister W.S. Fielding to put the bill aside. 'It seems to me that the directors of the bank should not be discharged. You have no conception of the criminal neglect of these men ... Giving them a discharge would be encouraging theft and robbery.'[16] The bill also met objections in the House of Commons. Dominique Monet was the deputy from the riding that included the town of St-Rémi, the site of a branch of the Banque du Peuple. He could not condone a discharge after many of his constituents had shown confidence that 'was chiefly grounded upon the solvency of the board of directors and upon [their] absolute liability.'[17] But Monet was very much in the minority and the bill passed the House. In the Senate it was amended, for Senator Macmillan, a bank shareholder, objected to the idea that any proceeds, after paying off the depositors, should go to the directors. In the amended version of the bill, these proceeds would go to the shareholders, but this was an academic issue since the assets yielded only $460,000.[18] With the directors providing their $200,000, the depositors had a final payment of nearly 75%, and the directors were off the hook.

The wrangling over the repayment of the depositors was partly a function of the peculiar organization of the Banque du Peuple. In any other chartered bank the rules of the Bank Act would have come into force with a liquidator paying off the depositors with the proceeds from the assets following the compensation of certain preferred creditors. However, the manoeuvring between 1895 and 1899 was also indicative of the emergence of a pool of savings within francophone Quebec capable of financing substantial banking operations. These savings were, in turn, used in large part to support numerous French-run enterprises, as is evident from the firms that collapsed in the wake of the fall of the Banque du Peuple. For instance, the St-Hyacinthe boot and shoe manufacturer, Séguin, Lalime et Compagnie, and the Montreal food processing firm of M. Lefebvre both closed following the bank's demise. Moreover, the vast majority of clients which had notes outstanding to the bank at the time of its suspension were French-speaking.[19] This was a bank which failed because of the mismanagement of the expanded resources at the disposal of francophone Quebecers.

III

The early history of the Banque Ville Marie is shrouded in a lack of information worthy of the Banque du Peuple. Most Canadian banks, including the Banque du Peuple, published their annual reports in local newspapers, but the Ville-Marie never adhered to this practice in the 1870s. Nevertheless, what is clear from the available information is that the bank was run by men seemingly oblivious to the economic circumstances of the 1870s. While the assets of all Canadian banks increased by less than 20% during 1874, the Ville-Marie saw its assets grow by over 75%, almost entirely because of the doubling of its current loans. Inevitably, many of these loans extended in the midst of a depression turned sour with the result that the Ville-Marie's overdue debts increased from $15,000 at the start of 1875 to $200,000 a year later. So seriously were its affairs compromised that a merger with the Metropolitan Bank was considered in the fall of 1876.[20]

Ultimately the bank chose to forego the merger and to continue with a revamped board of directors. By 1877 only one of the original directors remained, and four of the seven new leaders were men who had failed in their earlier attempt to establish the Banque St-Jean Baptiste. These new leaders operated much like their predecessors, expanding the Ville-Marie's assets by 50% between January 1877 and August 1879 while the industry as a whole saw assets shrink by nearly 10%. Once again, many loans could not be repaid, and, on the eve of its suspension in 1879, 21% of the bank's loans were overdue, compared to a figure of 6% for the industry.[21]

The Ville-Marie financed the expansion of its affairs by attracting deposits through branches that it established at St-Cuthbert, on the north shore of the St Lawrence across from Sorel, and at Trois-Rivières. In this regard, the bank ran ahead of the other French institutions that did not begin to tap the savings of francophones until the 1880s. As was the case with the Banque du Peuple, the Ville-Marie was able to report healthy profits, pay solid dividends, and tolerate bad loans as long as the deposits were coming in. However, by the spring of 1879 depositors' confidence was clearly waning in the wake of the suspension of the Mechanics Bank in late May, the Consolidated Bank in late July, and the Exchange Bank on 7 August. When a crowd of depositors materialized outside the head office of the Ville-Marie on 8 August, the bank had no choice but to suspend operations.[22]

The bank appeared to be on its way to liquidation. It reopened in early November so as to avoid the loss of its charter by virtue of the 'ninety-day' clause in the Bank Act, but the president, G.N. Dumesnil, explained to the shareholders that the loans through which the reopening was possible had only been secured 'à la condition que la banque liquiderait ses affaires.'[23] Dumesnil's days as president were numbered as reports emerged that the bank had borrowed substantial sums on the security of its own capital, had accepted dubious paper as security for bank stock, and had made loans worth over $1.2 million that were now valued at half that amount.[24] In January 1880 only three of the outgoing directors were re-elected, and the new board headed by Louis Archambault was committed to liquidation.

Archambault watched over the passing of legislation by parliament that set out the process for the liquidation of the Ville-Marie.[25] A meeting of shareholders was to be called to elect three liquidators, and this meeting was scheduled for 3 August, nearly one year after the suspension. But much to the surprise of Archambault and many of the shareholders, this meeting refused to appoint liquidators and instead chose, by a close vote, to re-establish the bank as a going concern. At a subsequent meeting in early 1881 the proponents of a return to normal operations brought in a report which estimated the market value of bank assets at $900,000 and which calculated that a reduction of the capital stock by $500,000 would be sufficient to purge bad debts and even start up a reserve fund.[26] For his part, Archambault argued that the assets were really worth less than $600,000. He also pointed out that the Ville-Marie was largely operating on funds borrowed at preferential rates from other banks, and he envisioned the day when high rates of interest might have to be paid: 'Alors il y aura désastre.'[27]

The shareholders were not interested in the gloom and doom being spread by Archambault, since the worst of the depression was over. They preferred a reduction of their investment by 50% to possibly losing it completely, and legislation to give effect to the reduction was passed early in 1881.[28] The shareholders must also have been encouraged to try to resume normal operations by the emergence in their midst of an experienced banker who appeared to have faith in the Ville-Marie. William Weir had been the head of the private banking firm of W. Weir and Company since 1849, and, although a Scot, he was no stranger to the francophone banks, having served as a director of the Banque Jacques-Cartier from 1878 to 1881 and as its vice-president during 1880 and 1881. In what was probably a speculative move, Weir acquired 252 shares of Ville-Marie stock during the course of 1880, a year in which the bank's future was far from certain. To become the bank's leading shareholder, Weir paid roughly $44 per share, a far cry from the $63 price being asked for before the suspension. Accordingly, he had little to lose if the bank were to resume operations with the face value of its stock effectively reduced from $100 to $50 per share. He was highly visible at the shareholders' meeting of January 1881 that resolved to make the reduction, as he moved several important resolutions, and at the next meeting in June of the same year he was elected as a director and was subsequently chosen to succeed Archambault as president. Weir was to hold this position until the bank's second and final suspension in 1899.

From 1881 to 1899 Weir operated the Banque Ville-Marie as if it were his private property. On the eve of the bank's demise he held on his own or in trust nearly one-quarter of the bank's stock in circulation. From this position of power he made life difficult for directors who did not see things his way. When Weir came to the bank all of the other directors were French-speaking, but they were gradually eased out, with Weir's English-speaking friends taking their place.[29] By 1894 there was not a single francophone on the board of directors, a situation that was not to change before 1899. At the same time Weir's cronies, such as Edward Lichtenheim and W.J. Withall, acquired large blocks of bank stock so that, by 1895, 65% of the shares in circulation were held by anglophones, a far cry from the 20% ten years earlier. Weir furthered his concentration of power by making himself cashier following Ubald Garand's resignation in 1892, and in the absence of any scrutiny over their actions Weir and his friends made substantial loans to firms that did not exist so as to gain the proceeds themselves. In other cases, they simply appropriated bank funds without even the pretence of a loan.[30] Following the bank's failure it took a jury only fifteen minutes to convict Weir of having submitted false reports to the government regarding bank affairs, and he was subsequently sentenced to two years in prison.

While Weir may have been an anglophone and a banker of

dubious repute, he saw to it that the Ville-Marie's operations were financed out of the savings of francophone Quebecers, as was the case for the other French banks of the period. Between 1881 and 1899 the number of branches increased from one to twenty, all located in overwhelmingly French communities. The bank carefully situated offices in towns without other banking facilities, with the result that Henri Bourassa could describe it in 1899 as having 'draw[n] more small capital from the farming community of the province than any other bank.'[31] The Ville-Marie's savings deposits increased from less than $300,000 in 1883 to more than $600,000 in 1893, and to over $1.25 million on the eve of its suspension. This last figure represented 57% of the bank's liabilities, only slightly less than the 58% recorded by the Banque Jacques-Cartier, which led all Quebec-based banks.

The Ville-Marie's branches also financed the bank's operations by facilitating the circulation of its notes. Weir noted in 1894, 'Au sujet des succursales nouvelles à établir, la banque a l'intention de se guider autant que possible d'après la circulation de ses billets, attendu que, sans la circulation de ses billets, les succursales de la campagne ne peuvent rapporter de bénéfices.'[32] But the circulation of bank notes under Weir surpassed all reasonable, or legal, bounds. By 1892 the note circulation stood at $475,000, a far cry from the $53,000 when he took command. At the same time the bank's unimpaired capital held by the public stood at only $375,000, which created a problem, as the Bank Act forebade the issuing of notes in excess of the value of paid capital.[33] The Department of Finance ordered Weir to reduce the note circulation, which he appeared to have done from the returns submitted to Ottawa.[34] In fact, however, the note circulation remained near the $500,000 level at the time of the suspension, even though only about half that amount was being reported.[35]

Weir needed to increase the bank's deposits rapidly and to expand its note circulation illegally in order to finance the bank's operations. By 1899 current loans and 'other assets,' the latter a euphemism employed to conceal certain dubious transactions, exceeded $1.65 million and accounted for nearly 75% of all assets

as opposed to the 61% figure for the industry as a whole. This was a bank with a small capital doing a large business, and one government official noted as early as 1892 that the Ville-Marie was 'trading on its note circulation and deposits.'[36] But owing to the dubious nature of many of Weir's loans this volume of operations did not bring about profits on a par with those of comparable banks. In fourteen of the nineteen years of Weir's leadership the Ville-Marie's profits ran below those recorded by Quebec banks of the same size. Nevertheless, in twelve of those years its dividends were superior to those of comparable banks, so Weir and his friends could at least be happy. The paying of handsome dividends meant that the Ville-Marie reserve fund could never exceed $20,000 and bad debts could not be written off the books.

The very existence of the Banque Ville-Marie was predicated on the steady expansion of the bank's deposits. In fact, curiously, Weir had often bragged that his bank made it a policy of lending out all of its deposits, so that any large-scale withdrawals could not possibly have been met.[37] Thus, when it was reported in the press that an official of the bank had stolen $58,000 and when depositors queued up to withdraw their funds, the bank was forced to close its doors on 25 July 1899.

This closure was greeted in the French press by lengthy articles making it clear that while the Ville-Marie may have had a French name it was really an English-run institution. The memory of the collapse of the Banque du Peuple was still fresh because of the long wrangling over the repayment of the depositors, and the bill to discharge the directors of further responsibility had only been passed earlier in the month. Accordingly, the French press sought to shore up confidence in the remaining French banks by stressing the Ville-Marie's Englishness. *La Presse* took the lead by noting that 'un financier bien connu a jeté la pierre aux Canadiens[-français] en disant que les banques canadiennes [-françaises] n'avaient pas de chance et qu'après la Banque du Peuple, c'était la Banque Ville-Marie. Faites-leur donc remarquer que la Banque Ville-Marie est une banque essentiellement anglaise. Ensuite rafraichez-leur la mémoire en leur appellant la dégringolade de la Metropolitan Banque, de l'Exchange Bank et de la Consolidated Bank, toutes banques anglaises.'[38] Both *La Presse* and *La Patrie* felt that the deposits of francophones had been deceitfully drawn to the Ville-Marie by its name, and they called upon their readers to patronize only the three truly French banks that were still doing business in Montreal.

The English press responded by arguing that the drawing of distinctions between French and English banks was 'unadulterated nonsense ... It makes very little difference to a bank manager whether his customer is English or French.'[39] But the question of language did seem to be of some importance to the Ville-Marie depositors, who were almost exclusively French and who stood to be the big losers in the whole affair. One depositor wrote to Laurier that he felt betrayed, having left his money in a bank with the 'nom trompeur Ville-Marie que nous croyons Banque Française.'[40]

This sense of betrayal was also expressed against the federal government, which had allowed the Ville-Marie to continue operations in spite of suspicions regarding its affairs. This outrage found its outlet through various *comités de vigilance* that surfaced across the province to protect the interests of depositors following the suspension. These committees held rallies and sent both petitions and deputations to Ottawa to seek relief, but to no avail. Some petitioners, such as those from Marieville who had placed $150,000 in the Ville-Marie, held Ottawa responsible, since its publication of bank returns had 'induit vos requérants à avoir confiance en cette banque et à y déposer leurs épargnes.'[41] The government had little sympathy with this argument. As the finance minister, W.S. Fielding, wrote, 'The government [can only] furnish the public with such information as can be obtained regarding the bank's affairs; they cannot accept any responsibility for the bank's affairs.'[42] Other petitioners argued that the government was responsible for having failed to check the bank's long-time practice of issuing excess notes. By virtue of the Bank Act the holders of Ville-Marie notes were compensated out of the realizable assets ahead of the depositors. The *Moniteur du Commerce* saw this simply as 'un vol de $300,000 au détriment des déposants,' but the government was unmoved.[43] When the liquidation of the bank was finally completed in 1905, the depositors were provided with roughly seventeen cents for each dollar they had entrusted to the Banque Ville-Marie.[44]

IV

Less than a week after the suspension of the Ville-Marie, another French bank was forced to close its doors. The run upon the Banque Jacques-Cartier was due to the fears of francophone depositors following the Ville-Marie fiasco, fears that some observers believed were heightened by all the talk in the French press about the need to support the remaining French banks. Nor was this the first time in the bank's history that a suspension had been required.

As the Jacques-Cartier entered 1875 it provided the appearance of a bank doing a sound business. It had a paid up capital of $2 million and assets that were reported as being worth over $5 million. In addition, the board of directors, which had barely changed since the bank's beginning, had managed to build up a reserve of $275,000 and to pay dividends that were generally above the norm for banks of its size. But just beneath the surface there was another side of the bank's affairs that few observed. Most ominous was the fact that it had long been earning profits below those gained by comparable Quebec banks. Its high dividends had been paid in 1874 out of the bank's capital, which is not entirely surprising in view of the revelations that came out after its suspension on 15 June 1875.[45] It came to light that the Jacques-Cartier's returns to the federal government had been regularly falsified since 1870 so as to conceal numerous dubious practices carried on by the cashier, Honoré Cotté. Among Cotté's sins were borrowing enormous sums from other banks at high rates of interest, granting substantial credit at low rates and with minimal security, and allowing considerable overdrafts by less than reliable clients.[46] The Jacques-Cartier became so dependent upon the support of other banks that 'the face of Mr. Cotté was as familiar to other bankers as that of their own customers.'[47]

Cotté was convicted in 1876 for having knowingly submitted

returns that placed the bank's assets at a figure $2.7 million above their real value. But the cashier was not alone in filling the vaults of the Jacques-Cartier with worthless paper. For instance, in the granting of over $600,000 in credit to Duncan Macdonald, the contractor for the Montreal Colonization Railway, Cotté had the support of the directors C.S. Rodier, J.L. Cassidy, and Jean-Baptiste Beaudry, who were also shareholders in the railway.[48] The banks that were supporting the Jacques-Cartier must have known that Macdonald's debts were due on 15 June 1875, a fact which led them in early June to demand a full investigation of the bank's affairs as a condition for further assistance.[49] Knowing what the result would be, the bank chose to close its doors on the same day that the debt was to come due.[50]

In early September, as the ninetieth day after the suspension approached, the bank resumed business so as to avoid the loss of its charter. No takers had been found for a merger with the Jacques-Cartier, and the reopening was merely a way of buying time so that means might be found to avoid a liquidation. It was to take until 1879 for the bank to right itself completely, a period during which no dividends were paid to shareholders who saw their investment cut in half in 1877 and in half again in 1879. The directors shared in the cost of the bank's mismanagement by paying $250,000 to the shareholders to gain a complete discharge for their failure to watch over Cotté.[51] By 1879 none of the original directors of the bank remained in office.

The province also had to come up with financial assistance to make the Jacques-Cartier a going concern once more. At the time of the suspension, the government of Quebec was the bank's leading creditor, with deposits of nearly $800,000. To save some of these funds the province provided the bank with $400,000 to adjust its account with Duncan Macdonald, whose viability was important to the government because it wanted to see the railway constructed. The provincial treasurer justified this assistance so as to protect 'hundreds of widows and orphans' whose savings might have been lost in the event of the bank's failure, but more likely he was concerned with the loss of his own deposits in the bank.[52]

With its bad debts purged from its books and the original directors purged from the administration, the bank once again resumed normal operations in 1879. It was now in a position to return to its proper vocation, the discounting of commercial paper 'particularly among its own shareholders.'[53] Between June 1879 and June 1880 the bank was able to pay dividends once again, and in the following year profits were set aside to re-establish the reserve fund.

The men who watched over this rebirth of the Jacques-Cartier generally fell into two categories. First, there were a number of English-speaking investors who acquired Jacques-Cartier stock at a pittance during the late 1870s. By 1881 English-speaking shareholders owned 40% of the bank's stock as opposed to their 20% in 1875. Among the bank's largest investors, anglophones owned half of the shares in 1881. These English investors become increasingly visible in the bank's affairs during its years of uncertainty. For instance, the six-member shareholders' committee that was appointed to look at the bank's books in May 1878 was equally divided between French and English members, but was to all intents and purposes run by the infamous William Weir. A subsequent committee which was formed later in 1878 had a majority of English speakers and submitted its report only in English. Then, at the bank's general meeting in January 1879 three of the seven directors elected were English.[54] Weir, who became vice-president of the bank in 1880, was joined by the long-time director J.L. Cassidy and the manufacturer Henry Jackson.

But this was as far as the anglicization of the Jacques-Cartier was to go. Weir soon left the bank to run the Banque Ville-Marie, and by the mid-1880s most of the other major investors had disposed of their stock, content with the profits they had made with their investment. Throughout the late 1870s Jacques-Cartier shares had been selling for roughly $7.50, but by 1883 this price reached $28.50. By 1884 the price had fallen to $20, and figuring that the peak had been reached the English investors sold their shares so that they controlled only 15% by 1884.[55] Accordingly, when Weir, Cassidy, and Jackson left the board they were not replaced by other English speakers.

Even at the height of their influence, however, the English investors had to share power with a new group of francophone businessmen that had entered bank affairs following the troubles of the 1870s. Leading this group was Alphonse Desjardins (not to be confused with the founder of the caisse populaire movement), who became president in 1879 and who held that post until 1899. While Desjardins was trained as a lawyer, he also had a vast array of business interests. As Paul-André Linteau has noted, 'Participant à la fois au capital foncier, industriel et financier, faisant le lien entre affaires et politique, Alphonse Desjardins est un exemple intéressant de membre de la moyenne bourgeoisie.'[56] By 1884 the English had largely abandoned the bank, and its board of directors was reduced to five members. Between that date and 1899 Desjardins was joined on the board by eight other men who, with the exception of the holdover Cassidy, were all francophones and all involved in a variety of business activities.

Under Desjardins' leadership the Jacques-Cartier set out to serve 'la classe mercantile et industrielle canadienne-française.'[57] That the bank saw its clientele as largely coming from the French community was evident from the nineteen branches that it established between 1879 and 1899. All but two of these were established in predominantly French communities within Quebec, but these two exceptions only made the orientation of the bank even clearer. In 1895 a branch was established in Edmonton whose goal was to serve 'l'élément canadien-français' of the region.[58] As for the branch located in Ottawa in 1898, it was, according to the directors, 'situated near the French Canadian commercial centre of the capital, and destined to render important services to our French-speaking countrymen.'[59] As had been the case with the Banque de Peuple and the Banque Ville-Marie, this expansion of the Jacques-Cartier's branches led to the mobilization of the savings of francophone Quebecers. By January 1899 the Jacques-Cartier's deposits amounted to over $3 million, which represented 58% of total liabilities, the highest figure recorded by a Quebec-based bank.

By and large the bank managed these funds responsibly. Its operations expanded rapidly in the early 1880s to allow the recording of both net profits and dividends above the norm for banks of its size. When an economic downturn set in in 1883 the bank's administration wisely froze the process by which assets had doubled since 1880, but with the bottoming out of the recession in 1885 a new period of expansion began that lasted until 1895 and saw a growth in assets of over 150% as opposed to only 45% for the industry as a whole. During this decade profits and dividends once more surpassed those of comparable banks. A further recession struck in 1895, but it was adequately handled by the Jacques-Cartier, which tightened up on credit and closed down seven branches. Under its new cashier, Tancrède Bienvenu, the bank experienced another spurt of growth between June 1897 and June 1899. The Jacques-Cartier's assets increased by over 50%, more than twice the rate for the industry in general, and its profits again outstripped those reported by Quebec banks of its size.

The directors announced sound profits, a reasonable dividend, and an increase in the bank's reserve fund to $265,000 at its annual meeting in June 1899; there was little reason to believe that the Jacques-Cartier would be closed within six weeks. The run by depositors that began after the collapse of the Ville-Marie struck only two banks, the Jacques-Cartier and the Banque d'Hochelaga, both of which were French institutions whose head offices were situated in Montreal. There was nothing in particular about the management of either bank that prompted the panic, only an irrational fear promoted by the Ville-Marie fiasco. Bienvenu was prophetic in having idly commented to Laurier in June 1899 that 'le défaut principal [de la Banque Jacques-Cartier] aux yeux de certains gens c'est qu'elle est trop canadienne-française.'[60]

Once the run began the Jacques-Cartier was not able to continue operations, having already repaid $1.5 million, and with still other depositors waiting at its door. Thus, the suspension was necessary. Like other Canadian banks the Jacques-Cartier was highly dependent upon depositors' savings to operate, but only a small percentage of these funds were held in the form of liquid assets. E.P. Neufeld has defined a bank's liquidity ratio as 'Canadian and foreign cash items and Government of Canada securities as a proportion of chartered bank note and deposit

TABLE 3.1
Liquidity of Quebec banks with total assets of $5–10 million, 30
June 1899

Bank	Liquidity ratio (%)
Banque d'Hochelaga	32
Banque Nationale	7
Banque Jacques-Cartier	9
Eastern Townships Bank	5

Source: See appendix I.

liabilities.'[61] On this basis the Jacques-Cartier was slightly better off than two of the comparable Quebec banks, the Banque Nationale and the Eastern Townships Bank, neither of which had to face the panic. By contrast, the Jacques-Cartier's liquidity ratio was much lower than that recorded by the Hochelaga, which helps to explain why the latter bank survived the run so effortlessly. Nevertheless, Bienvenu's management of the bank was so close to the norm that he was kept on after the suspension and given a strong hand to reorganize its affairs. Of the administrators, only Desjardins was forced to step aside, and this was because of his own inability to repay a personal debt of $100,000.[62]

In his strengthened role Bienvenu's first task was to do what was needed so as to avoid a forced liquidation because of the ninety-day clause. To reopen before the end of October, he sold off most of the bank's remaining branches, borrowed considerable sums from other banks, and sought pledges from depositors that they would leave their money in the bank for a year. To intimidate recalcitrant depositors, Bienvenu wrote the following letter in early October: 'Je suis chargé de vous informer que si, d'ici au 15 octobre, vous n'avez pas signé le document accordant une extension de délai à la Banque Jacques-Cartier, pour le remboursement de vôtre dépôt, la Banque devra nécessairement liquider. En ce cas, vous devrez seul assumer l'entière responsabilité des pertes qui vous pourriez subir, les directeurs ayant fait tout leur possible pour éviter un pareil malheur.'[63] All of the depositors evidently did not fall in line, for $600,000 of deposits were withdrawn during the month following the bank's reopening on 25 October. Bienvenu's agent in Ottawa pointed out that many depositors refused to sign because they had read reports in the newspaper that the reopening was guaranteed whether they signed or not; by not signing they could then immediately get their money back in full.[64] But in spite of these holdouts the bank was able to resume business.

The long-term course for the bank was laid out by its new president, G.N. Ducharme, at a meeting of directors in early December. Ducharme reported that the bank's bad loans could be covered simply through the appropriation of the reserve fund. However, to relaunch operations in a serious way the bank needed to increase its capital from the $500,000 figure that had been in place since 1879. This new capital would not be forthcoming in the absence of a reserve fund which might act as a guarantee to potential investors that their shares would be reasonably secure. Accordingly, Ducharme proposed that the existing capital be reduced by half so as to set free $250,000 for the re-establishment of the reserve fund. Subsequently, a further $750,000 in capital would be sought to bring the total to $1 million. The president left no doubt that he wanted Bienvenu to execute this plan. The general manager's salary was increased to $5,000 and he was to receive a $10,000 bonus if he could raise $250,000 in new capital.[65]

Bienvenu resorted to several expedients in order to gain these new funds. Between December 1899 and July 1900 he tried to convince depositors to translate their savings into bank stock, announced that a savings department would be established to invest all savings of less than $1,000 in call loans with good guarantees, and promised that loans to directors would be henceforth forbidden.[66] He also insisted that the bank change its name to the Banque Provinciale du Canada so that new investors would feel no uneasiness about buying stock in a bank that had twice suspended operations and had reduced its capital by 50% on three separate occasions. Apparently these manoeuvres worked, and the shareholders of the Banque Jacques-Cartier met for the last time on 6 July 1900. Three days later the Banque Provinciale opened for business.

v

The Banque Nationale and the Banque d'Hochelaga survived the summer of 1899 intact for very different reasons: the former because of good fortune and the latter because of an extremely cautious management. The good fortune of the Nationale was partly related to the location of its head office in Quebec City, which helped shield it from the panic of depositors. It was doubly lucky that this weakening of depositors' confidence had not taken place earlier in the century when its operations were unprofitable, to say the least.

At the start of the depression of the 1870s the Banque Nationale was the largest of the French banks, owing to its considerable activity in the timber trade. This activity meant that the bank operated much like the other Quebec City–based banks. So, as the Nationale opened it first branches in the early 1870s at Ottawa, Montreal, and Sherbrooke, it was with an eye towards timber accounts. With the deepening of the depression the timber trade came to a standstill, and the bank found itself with clients who could not repay their large loans. The reserve fund of $400,000 was appropriated between 1876 and 1881 to cover these losses, but still bad debts remained on the books which compromised the bank's affairs. Between 1882 and 1887 a further $600,000 in bad debts was purged, which required the paying of only intermittent dividends to the shareholders. The bank's profits consistently ran below the norm for Quebec institutions of its size, so withholding funds from shareholders was the only answer. In 1888 the very investment of the shareholders was slashed by 40% so as to set free $800,000. Still, it was only in 1893 that the bank could finally announce that it had disposed of the last of the timber limits that had fallen into its hands.[67] In the following year it was able to report profits that were above the norm for comparable banks for only the second time in a decade.

From the 1870s through to the early 1890s the Nationale's leaders failed to change the nature of the business, no matter how poor the profits and how great the losses. The bank did a very small volume of business, its assets actually shrinking by 30% between 1875 and 1892. The leaders continued to depend upon the timber trade in spite of its vulnerability to changes in the international economy, at the same time ignoring the possibility of expanding their business by opening branches through which deposits might be secured. While the other French banks were busy mobilizing the savings of francophone Quebecers, the administrators of the Banque Nationale were sitting on their hands, opening no new branches between 1875 and 1893. As a result, by 1888 only 11% of its liabilities were being derived from savings deposits, roughly half the percentage for all Quebec banks of its size. *Le Prix Courant* urged the bank to follow 'l'exemple donné par la Banque du Peuple d'aller chercher les dépôts en établissant des succursales à la portée des déposants; de donner plus d'étendue au territoire couvert par sa circulation ... C'est avec les dépôts et la circulation que l'on gagne de dividendes aux actionnaires.'[68] One of these shareholders noted the result of the failure to expand the bank's business at the 1889 general meeting: 'Avec un capital de $1 million [la Banque du Peuple] fait des affaires pour $5 million. Ici, avec un capital de $1.2 million les opérations ne se chiffrent que pour $2 million.'[69]

Despite these calls for change, the bank only moved to expand its operations following the disposal of the last timber limits in 1893. Joseph Thibaudeau's presidency (1879–89) was marked by constant complaints from shareholders about his policies.[70] He was ultimately chased from office, as was his successor Auguste Gaboury (1889–95).[71] It was only under the leadership of Rodolphe Audette (1895–1921) that the bank firmly committed itself to its expansionist course. In all, fifteen branches were established during the 1890s, and many more were to come in the new century. All but one of these fifteen were established in predominantly French communities in Quebec. In the exceptional case a branch was opened in Winnipeg, but it was soon closed because of the difficulties of a French bank trying to crack an English market. These branches allowed the bank's deposits to increase by 60% between 1893 and 1899 and its assets to grow by 40%. By the turn of the century savings deposits accounted for 40% of the bank's liabilities, a far cry from the 11% a decade earlier; with this expanded business the Nationale was able to earn profits above those for Quebec banks of its size. If dividends were still not up to the norm, it was only because a reserve fund was being built up which stood at $150,000 by 1899.

Curiously, at the same time that the bank was finally becoming profitable, a group of its shareholders was selling off its stock. Ever since the early years of the bank, a significant block of shares had been held by English investors who were often attracted by the Nationale's ties with the timber trade. In 1891, 25% of the bank's shares were held by English-speakers, but while the number of shares in circulation remained unchanged over the next decade the percentage in the hands of anglophones fell to 10% by 1901. Many of these investors had retained their shares throughout the years of poor dividends; if they had been overly concerned about earning a good return on their investment they would have sold off their stocks well before the 1890s. Thus, it is unlikely that they pulled out of the bank simply because they were now able to sell their stock at a better price. Rather, they were abandoning a bank that had finally liquidated its ties to the timber trade and was now focusing upon rural Quebec. Their actions were mirrored in the resignation from the board of directors of H.M. Price and Richard Turner in 1895. Both were tied to the timber trade, and following their departure lumber interests would never again be seen on the board of the Nationale, and no English-speaker would hold a seat again until 1922.

By the turn of the century, the Banque Nationale, like the Jacques-Cartier, had seen its once-significant group of English investors replaced by French shareholders. Moreover, the vaults of the Nationale were filled with the savings of francophone Quebecers, as those of the Jacques-Cartier had been prior to the panic of 1899. Considering its low liquidity ratio, the same fate probably would have awaited the Banque Nationale had its head office been located in Montreal. The Nationale operated throughout its history with the burden of being situated in Quebec City, whose day as a leading business centre had passed. In this one case, however, the bank was fortunate to have been based in the old capital.

By contrast, there was no luck involved in the ease with which the Banque d'Hochelaga survived the panic of 1899. Depositors lined up in front of the offices of the Hochelaga, as they did before all the French banks based in Montreal, but it was only at the Hochelaga that the run was met with an air of confidence. The *Montreal Star* described the scene as follows: 'Heaps of gold piled up beside the paying teller of whom three extra were added to accommodate the demands of the situation, were tangible evidence to show that the bank was prepared for all demands upon it. The confident air of the officials and the prompt payment of all claims were factors that could not be disregarded and many who came to withdraw their money went away leaving it in the bank's keeping. And there were also numerous large depositors who in full view of the crowds present, handed their money into the receiving window with an air of confidence.'[72] Nor was there any reason why either the bank or its customers should have felt any concern. The Hochelaga had a liquidity ratio of 32%, well above the industry average of 20%. This left it with nearly $4 million of immediately realizable assets and total deposits that barely exceeded that figure. The bank's general manager, Marie-Joseph-Alfred Prendergast, had been criticized some months earlier for having managed the bank's funds in an overly conservative manner, but the events of summer 1899 allowed Prendergast to have the last laugh.[73]

Conservatism had been the watchword of Hochelaga policy from the bank's inception in the mid-1870s. While other banks rapidly increased their paid-up capital so as to expand their note circulation, the Hochelaga moved slowly to reach its authorized level of $1 million only in 1898. The bank took part in the mobilization of the savings of francophone Quebecers by establishing thirteen branches, eleven of which were situated in the province. Still, it turned down an even greater number of requests from towns eager for branches, so by 1899 its savings deposits accounted for only 48% of total liabilities, the average for Quebec banks of its size. The Hochelaga handled these funds in a safe manner, never tying them up in any one sector and certainly not in an industry as vulnerable to the uncertainties of international commerce as the lumber trade. The Hochelaga had easy access to funds in 1899 since only 55% of its total assets were tied up in current loans, a figure well below the norm for comparable banks.

This model of conservative banking was ruled over by a small number of men, nearly all of whom were francophone business-men. Heading this group was F. X. St-Charles, a merchant and private banker, who served as president from 1879 to 1909. There was little apparent dissatisfaction with either St-Charles or the rest of the directors, whose average term during this period was longer than that for the directors of any other Quebec bank, and this includes the Banque du Peuple, whose directors were free from the scrutiny of shareholders. Nor was there any reason why the Hochelaga's shareholders should have been displeased with St-Charles and his colleagues. The depression of the 1870s was not easy for the recently opened bank, and in early 1879 it briefly considered merging with the Banque Jacques-Cartier.[74] The bank's situation was hardly aided by the revelation in the same year that its cashier had absconded with $85,000. Ultimately, dividends had to be suspended for two years and the reserve fund had to be appropriated so that the Hochelaga might right itself. Then, with St-Charles in place as president and with some new tough rules regarding the granting of loans, the bank pros-pered throughout the 1880s and 1890s.[75] In only four of these twenty years did profits fall below the norm for Quebec banks of the Hochelaga's size. At the same time dividends hovered around the average for comparable banks, thus allowing the building up of a reserve fund of $565,000 by 1899. Owing to steady growth, the Hochelaga became the largest French bank following the demise of the Banque du Peuple, and as the century came to a close it was about to become the first such bank to reach the $10-million mark in total assets.

Under these circumstances, it is little wonder that the Hoche-laga could face the panic of 1899 with confidence. Still, St-Charles was taking no chances as he asked the Archbishop of Montreal to issue a public letter urging depositors to leave their money in the French banks.[76] Archbishop Bruchési gladly complied with this request, and further, but this time unsolicited, support came from the Bank of British North America. The general manager also received a letter from the Hochelaga's New York bankers urging him to draw upon them for as much support as he needed. But the bank's position was so sound that Prendergast was later able to comment: 'Nous n'avons pas eu besoin d'accepter cette offre.'[77]

At the turn of the century the Banque d'Hochelaga was the Cadillac of French banking. Because of its conservative bent it never received the adulation in the press that had been reserved for the Banque du Peuple in the late 1880s and early 1890s. Nevertheless, among businessmen, French and English alike, there was great respect for the bank. The English business establishment of Montreal showed its acceptance by choosing Prendergast (a francophone in spite of his name) to be the president of the bankers' section of the Montreal Board of Trade in 1898, the first official of a French bank to hold that post. Further evidence of English business support came in the form of a substantial increase in the stock held by the Montreal City and District Savings Bank. The City and District included on its board of directors such leading lights of the Montreal business scene as J.H.R. Molson and A.F. Gault, and between 1881 and 1901 it increased its investment in the Hochelaga from $45,600 to $286,700. But this one institutional investor aside, almost all of the increase in the Hochelaga's capital over these twenty years from $685,000 to $1.5 million came out of the pockets of French investors. Their support was a vote of confidence for the management of St-Charles and Prendergast, but it was also indicative of the greater savings in the hands of francophones that was a factor in the operations of all the French banks during this period.

VI

The business practices of the French banks of Montreal and Quebec City ran the gamut of possibilities during the last quarter of the nineteenth century from the conservative behaviour of the Banque d'Hochelaga to the rapid expansion of the Banque du Peuple and the Banque Ville-Marie. Some, like the Jacques-Cartier, seemed prone to crises, while the Banque Nationale, for all its problems, escaped a suspension of its operations. This same diversity was also evident among the smaller English banks of the province's two major centres. While institutions such as the Mechanics Bank and the Stadacona Bank quickly exited from the scene, the Union Bank and the Quebec Bank continued to operate throughout the period. However, while the former bank greatly expanded its operations by extending its business to the prairies, the latter languished with little growth and weak profits. As a result of this diversity on each side of the language line, when one controls for the size of the bank there was little difference during this period between the French and English banks of Quebec either in terms of the structure of their assets and liabilities or in the profitability of their affairs.[78]

The size of the bank, while more closely related than language to the operations of the institution, could not explain all of the differences that emerged between institutions. Certainly among the French banks there were considerable differences among institutions of a similar size. These differences were the product of a variety of less quantifiable factors, such as the history of the bank and the connections and predilections of its leaders. Regardless of these differences, however, what did distinguish the French banks during this period was their ability, not evident prior to 1875, to finance their operations out of the savings of francophone Quebecers. They were able to keep pace with the other Quebec banks of their size, which were increasingly depending upon savings deposits as a source of loanable funds, by establishing numerous branches across rural Quebec. During the 1880s, for instance, twenty of the twenty-two new branches established in the province were opened by the French banks, and just prior to the panic of 1899 their savings deposits totalled $11.7 million, a far cry from the $3.25 million at the start of 1875. These branches also provided the means by which capital could be secured for the French banks. The Banque Ville-Marie, for instance, made the purchase of bank stock by local citizens a condition for the opening of its first branches to the north of Montreal in the late 1870s. As a result, by 1881, nearly $200,000 had been invested in the bank by residents of the region. By 1891 the Ville-Marie had largely shifted its branch operations to the area south of Montreal so that nearly 25% of its reported capital came from that region.

These banks also gained considerable capital from the well-to-do men who sat on their boards of directors. Between 1875 and 1899 the majority of the directors were francophone merchants, who were clearly wealthier and possessed a wider array of business connections than had their predecessors from the pre-1875 period.[79] Take the example of the Banque du Peuple. Its first president, Louis-Michel Viger, was a merchant who did not seem to have any other business connections of note, while its last leader, Jacques Grenier, could boast directorships in the Montreal Cotton Company and Dominion Cotton Mills to go along with his own commercial enterprises. In the affairs of the Banque Jacques-Cartier, there was a similar transition from the merchant Jean-Louis Beaudry to the omnipresent Alphonse Desjardins. The French banks were able to secure additional investment capital both from these men and through their new branches with the result that the percentage of their capital under the control of francophones greatly increased during the period.

While table 3.2 reflects the increasing 'francization' of the capital stock of the French banks, it also reflects their vulnerability. The shrinkage of the total capital between 1881 and 1901 was the result of reductions in the capital stock of some of the banks along with the collapse of two of them in the 1890s. In fact, the disappearance of the anglicized Banque du Peuple and Banque Ville-Marie played a role in the increase of the percentage of stock controlled by francophones between 1891 and 1901. Like other small banks in Canada, the French banks were highly susceptible to recessions and the poor management of administrators trying to do a large business on a small capital. Accordingly, the percentage of Canadian bank assets controlled by the French banks at the start of 1900 was only half of what it had been in 1875. Nevertheless, the growth that all of these banks achieved at some

TABLE 3.2
French investment in the French banks, 1871–1901

	Total capital in French banks (million $)	% held by Francophones
1871	5.49	61.5
1881	6.67	65.0
1891	5.09	71.9
1901	4.56	85.6

Source: See appendix II.

point during this period indicated the existence of savings in francophone Quebec upon which the surviving banks could build in the new century.

4

The Small-town Banks: 1873–1908

I

The banks of Montreal and Quebec City, English and French alike, operated across relatively large territories in their search for loanable funds and in their effort to satisfy their most important clients. While French banks were hardly visible in international dealings during the nineteenth century, they did make several efforts to expand beyond Quebec, and within the province their operations spanned thousands of square miles. However, the Canadian banking system also consisted of banks whose vocation was to provide services to a much more restricted area. These banks were largely formed by merchants and other businessmen of secondary urban centres who sought to mobilize local capital, often for the support of projects which they headed.

The expansion of the banking system during the early 1870s gave rise to such small-town institutions as the Pictou Bank in Nova Scotia, the Western Bank in Oshawa, and the two French entries – the Banque de St-Jean and the Banque de St-Hyacinthe. By 1881 there were ten such banks with total assets of $14 million. The following decade saw the beginning of their demise with the Ontario Bank moving from Bowmanville to Toronto and the failure of the Pictou Bank. It was the first decade of the new century, however, that witnessed the rapid decline of these tiny institutions. By the end of 1912 the only bank in Canada whose

TABLE 4.1
Local capital and the small-town banks, 1901

	St-Hyacinthe	St-Jean	Sherbrooke	Trois-Rivières
Population	9,210	4,030	11,765	9,981
Total bank investment	$296,363	$203,363	$331,718	$145,915
Investment in local bank	$284,300	$143,000	$239,900	–
Total investment per capita	$32.18	$50.40	$28.20	$14.61

Source: *Census of Canada*, 1901; Canada, *Sessional Papers*, no. 6, 1901

headquarters was not in a major centre was the Weyburn (Saskatchewan) Security Bank with total assets of less than $1.2 million.

The rise and fall of the small-town banks of Quebec paralleled the pattern elsewhere in Canada. By 1874 the Banque de St-Jean, the Banque de St-Hyacinthe, and the Sherbrooke-based Eastern Townships Bank were all in operation, the product of local interests seeking to mobilize capital for local projects. The success of these banks in mobilizing this capital is evident in table 4.1. In the three minor Quebec towns which housed bank head offices, the vast majority of investment in bank stocks went to the local institutions. In Trois-Rivières, where the idea of establishing a bank was repeatedly rejected, the per capita investment in bank shares was considerably lower.

But here the similarity between the two French banks and their English counterpart ends. By 1912 all three had passed from the scene, but in very different fashions. All of Canada's small-town banks suffered from the restricted nature of their operations, which made them particularly vulnerable to bad management, recessions, and the designs of the larger banks, but this was particularly the case for the smallest of the French banks, whose operations were further circumscribed by language. Both of the French banks failed in 1908, but while the fate of the Banque de

St-Jean was sealed by the wrongdoings of its leaders, the Banque de St-Hyacinthe might have had a future had it had access to further sources of capital. For its part, the Eastern Townships Bank was able to gain needed financing from English interests who resided beyond the region before its acquisition by the Canadian Bank of Commerce in 1912. The contrast between the Banque de St-Hyacinthe and the Eastern Townships Bank points to the limited capital market within which all French banks operated.

II

The Banque de St-Jean should probably never have seen the light of day. When it began operations in 1873 it most likely had less than the capital required by law and was situated in a town whose economy was going nowhere. Nor did the St-Jean economy pick up during the next thirty-five years. The town failed to attract any industry of note until the arrival of the Singer sewing machine factory just after the turn of the century, and it never emerged as an agricultural service centre of any great importance.[1] As a result, St-Jean's population in 1901 barely exceeded 4,000, 15% less than it had been in 1891. Under these circumstances one might have hoped that the bank would quietly pass from the scene, inconveniencing as few people as possible. Unfortunately, this was not to be the case.

Through the issuing of notes which were no doubt illegal, because of the dubious nature of its paid capital, the bank did a sufficient business to survive the depression of the 1870s and even to show respectable profits during the early 1880s.[2] By 1884 it had even managed to establish a reserve fund of $10,000. The recession of 1885 struck the bank hard, however, and for the next decade it appeared that it was slowly moving towards liquidation. During that decade an annual dividend of more than 2% was only paid twice. Moreover, the note circulation shrank by 80%, deposits by 70%, and total assets by 40%. In 1883 *Le Moniteur du Commerce* described how 'cette banque continue graduellement à descendre de la scène ... Il n'y a pas à St-Jean les éléments d'une banque; celle-ci n'était née viable; et à vrai dire, elle n'a jamais été qu'une ombre de banque. Grâce à l'exiguité de ses opérations elle ne fait que peu de risques, et nous croyons qu'elle se tirera d'affaires sans faire perdre personne.'[3] Nor would the disappearance of the bank have bothered the Department of Finance. The deputy minister wrote in 1893 that 'the bank has deposits from the public of about $62,000, on which it is trading, and it is clear that the public have no great confidence in the institution.'[4]

The early exit of the Banque de St-Jean was put off by the failure of the Banque du Peuple in 1895. The latter bank had probably played a role in the reduction of the Banque de St-Jean's operations between 1885 and 1895 through its circulation of bank notes and collection of deposits throughout the region. At the time of its collapse the Banque du Peuple had $375,000 in deposits from its branches at St-Jean and nearby St-Rémi, but with the passing of this bank a market suddenly opened up which the Banque de St-Jean might serve.[5] During July 1895, the month of the Banque du Peuple's collapse, the Banque de St-Jean increased its note circulation by 50%, and in the course of the year its deposits increased by the same percentage. It even acquired the Banque du Peuple's building at St-Jean so as to have a more spacious head office.[6]

The Banque de St-Jean was untouched by the hysteria that struck the French banks of Montreal in 1899, and up to its closing in April 1908 it continued to expand its note circulation and savings deposits, aided by the opening of three branches in the region. In order to expand its source of loanable funds, the bank did not try to increase the amount of its capital that was subscribed, nor did it seek further payment upon shares already subscribed. By 1908 only $316,000 was reported to have been paid on its $500,000 of subscribed capital, but there were few in the finance department who believed that even that amount had really been paid.

The funds that the bank collected from the public seem to have gone, for the most part, to support the various interests of P.H. Roy, its second president. Throughout the last quarter of the nineteenth century, the bank was administered by a small group of local merchants and professional men, most of whom were francophones and who were led by Louis Molleur, a long-time Liberal deputy in the Legislative Assembly. Molleur was the bank's only president until Roy, his son-in-law, succeeded him in 1904, prompting the *Monetary Times* to call the bank 'a family affair.'[7] But Roy, a Montreal lawyer and Liberal deputy in Quebec City, had an association with the bank that predated his term as president or even his first election as a director in 1902. Roy had held 200 of the bank's 5,000 shares throughout the 1880s, but he increased his personal holdings to 850 in 1893 and to 1,063 in 1895. With his wife taking on an additional 250 shares, by January 1896 Roy was the leading investor in the bank as it took on new life following the Banque du Peuple's demise. Just as William Weir packed the administration of the Banque Ville-Maire, so too Roy brought his cronies, usually Montrealers, to share in the spoils of the Banque de St-Jean. Montrealers held the majority of seats on the board of directors of this small-town bank by 1908, and in that year Roy further assured freedom from scrutiny by making himself the general manager.

Roy pushed local interests out of the way so as to operate the bank for his own profit. In the late 1890s he used his control of the bank's capital to gain financing for the construction of the East Richelieu Valley Railway, of which he was the president and promoter. The railway that was to be built from Iberville, which was across the Richelieu River from St-Jean, to a point near the American border was chartered in 1891 and completed in 1898. The bank eventually loaned the railway $350,000, but there is no evidence that any of this money was ever repaid; nor did the bank ever report this overdue debt in its monthly returns to the government.[8] In other cases Roy and his friends appropriated bank funds without even the pretence of a loan. A federal justice ministry official noted shortly after the bank's suspension: 'For twelve or fourteen years, possibly more, its funds have been systematically withdrawn by Mr. Roy for his own purposes and projects upon the discount of worthless paper put through by his directors. The other directors and officers appear to have been his supine tools, and some of the former, at least, were interested in his schemes. The result is to wipe out about $650,000 of the bank's alleged assets [of nearly $1 million] ... So late as 18 April 1908 [ten days before the suspension], Mr. Roy withdrew $10,000 in cash.'[9]

Roy, and Molleur before him, kept suspicion away from the bank and kept deposits in its vaults by paying respectable annual dividends of 6% from 1900 to 1906. The public no doubt assumed that these dividends were being paid out of profits, but no one could be certain; the bank had long made it a practice of not publishing its annual reports. In the light of subsequent revelations about the real value of the bank's assets, however, it is unlikely that dividends were paid out of profits. Rather, they were probably paid out of the deposits held by the bank so as to gratify Roy and his friends.

The bank's leaders were so successful in covering their tracks that the suspension of the bank in April 1908 was seen simply as an action prompted by the competition provided by larger banks. There was no run on the bank by uneasy depositors, and *Le Moniteur du Commerce* stressed that 'cette liquidation [était] purement volontaire.'[10] Ostensibly this was true. Neither the federal government nor the Canadian Bankers' Association seems to have been pressing for the bank's closure, which says something about their success as guardians of the public's funds. Roy must have felt that he had taken all from the bank that he could get away with, and that a voluntary suspension would gain him a sympathetic hearing by federal officials. But if this was his assumption, he was quite wrong. The bank closed on 28 April, on 12 May the directors began the liquidation procedures, and by July Roy was facing a preliminary hearing on charges of falsifying returns to the government. Ever the crafty operator, Roy delayed his trial until the following May through a series of requests for a change in venue.[11] Once the trial began, however, there was little he could do to stop the emergence of unflattering evidence, such as the fact that he had cashed worthless notes with a value of nearly $575,000.[12] Roy tried to bring an end to the trial by committing suicide, but since he only managed to wound himself in the foot the trial continued. He was sentenced to five years in prison where he died in 1910.

While Roy was manoeuvring to escape punishment and while

the few solvent shareholders were doing all they could to escape their double liability to creditors, it became clear that the depositors of the Banque de St-Jean were going to see little, if any, of the $360,000 owed to them.[13] The bank had gained these funds from francophone Quebecers who also helped finance the operations of the French banks of Montreal and Quebec City, but the bank's assets were worth so little that after paying off the preferred creditors there was little left for the depositors. Many residents of St-Jean and St-Rémi, who had earlier lost some of their savings with the collapse of the Banque du Peuple, now saw most of the their savings evaporate with the demise of the Banque de St-Jean.[14]

III

Just as the suspension of the Banque Ville-Marie triggered the run on the French banks of Montreal in 1899, the closing of the Banque de St-Jean gave rise to a similar excitement on the plain to the south of Montreal. The Banque de St-Jean and the Banque de St-Hyacinthe had long been associated with each other in the public's mind, whether rightly or wrongly. Both emerged at roughly the same time and pursued businesses that were restricted to the same area of the province. Accordingly, the suspension of the Banque de St-Jean in April 1908 led to a withdrawal of funds from the Banque de St-Hyacinthe which played a role in the latter's closing in June.

This comparison is not entirely fair to the Banque de St-Hyacinthe, however. While the bank certainly had its share of problems, its leaders were never accused of a misappropriation of funds, for they operated in a city whose economy was much more buoyant than was St-Jean's. In fact, by 1895 St-Hyacinthe had become the province's fourth largest city, owing to its importance both as a commercial and industrial centre. Its commercial significance was linked to the transformation of the region into an important area for dairy farming, a fact that was symbolized by the establishment of the provincial government's dairy school at St-Hyacinthe in 1892. The growth of industry was also important to the city's development: the number of industrial workers increased by over 500% between 1871 and 1901 with capital investment increasing by nearly 900%.[15]

Local interests played a key role in this process of growth. St-Hyacinthe entrepreneurs headed up a number of the major industries, often supported by the municipal government, which provided over $250,000 in various forms of aid to support industrial growth. Similarly active was the Banque de St-Hyacinthe. Its annual reports never failed to note the amount of support provided to the dairy industry, but closer to the hearts of the bank's directors was the financing of local industrial projects. This is hardly surprising in the light of the composition of its board of directors. For instance, five future directors of the bank were among the six men who organized the Compagnie Manufacturière de St-Hyacinthe in 1873. Leading this group was G.C. Dessaulles, who served as the bank's president from 1878 to 1908. The bank was not long in operation before the Compagnie Manufacturière was seeking credit to operate its woollen mill and to develop the city's water power, which was largely under its control. In 1878 the bank, under Dessaulles' not altogether disinterested leadership, voted a blank cheque of support for the company, and in 1881 it refinanced the firm's debts with payment only due in six years.[16] The bank also became deeply involved in the affairs of Feodor Boas, who came to St-Hyacinthe to operate a textile mill using the water power of the Compagnie Manufacturière, but who ended up as the proprietor of the company and one of the largest clients of the bank. Boas, who also became a major investor in Banque de St-Hyacinthe stock, repeatedly returned to the bank to refinance his various debts and by 1898 owed $330,000 to a bank whose paid capital was only $312,000.[17]

As long as these various industries were able to stay afloat, the local economy could expand and the bank could report sound profits. By 1894 Boas' Granite Mills were employing eight hundred workers and the Séguin-Lalime shoe factory, another firm aided by the bank to the tune of $75,000, was giving work to five hundred. In the midst of this growth the local press could not contain its enthusiasm and commented: 'Nous sommes heureux et fiers de voir que pendant que les ouvriers dans les autres villes chôment, les industries à St-Hyacinthe grandissent et que partout la ville progresse d'une manière étonnante. En avant toujours!'[18] The bank's annual reports displayed the same booster spirit, and with good reason, for it consistently recorded profits well above those for comparable banks up to the mid-1890s. The bank was able to pay sound dividends throughout this period, and had managed to build up a reserve fund of $75,000 by 1898.

However, by the mid-1890s both St-Hyacinthe industry and the bank were entering a rough period. Between 1898 and 1902 the population of the city declined by 13%, mostly because of large-scale layoffs at the major industries. The Séguin-Lalime factory had reduced its work force to two hundred by 1901, and closed in the following year. As for the Granite Mills, similar reductions occurred prior to its shutdown in 1899. These failures could not have come as much of a surprise to the bank, which had been repeatedly asked to refinance the debts of its industrial clients, most notably those of Boas' various firms. These debts were reorganized in 1899 when the Boas properties were taken over by an American syndicate under the name of the Canadian Woollen Mills. In return for the $300,000 which it was owed, the bank agreed to accept $54,000 in cash with the rest in various stocks and bonds of the new firm. Most of the cash payment was wiped out when the bank was required to advance $30,000 for 'reorganization expenses' and to guarantee $50,000 of the new company's bonds.[19] By 1901 the president of the firm, J.G. Cannon, was already seeking an extension on the loan and was anticipating a suspension of interest payments on the bonds because of the difficulties of the mill.[20] By 1902 the company was in liquidation and the bank had accepted a final settlement for its nearly $100,000 in bonds, leaving it with less than $50,000 to show for its $300,000 investment in the various mills.[21]

Unfortunately for the bank this was not its only large and unprofitable investment. It became involved with the United Counties Railway through one of its long-time directors, Michel Bernier, who was also the railway's chief promoter. By 1896 the railway had been completed from Sorel to Iberville via St-Hyacinthe, but only by means of an ever-growing line of credit from the bank. This debt reached $500,000 by 1900, a sum that one observer described as 'plus que le permettait son capital.'[22] In order to recoup its investment the bank pushed for the sale of the railway to a solvent operator, and in 1900 Dessaulles acquired the line in the bank's name with the understanding that the railway would be subsequently transferred to an American syndicate for $500,000 in cash and bonds. The transfer took place and the line became part of the Quebec Southern Railway, but the bank was going to have to wait a long time for payment.[23] In 1904 the directors had to report that 'la créance de la Banque contre le Québec Southern n'est pas encore réglée.'[24] In fact, the railway was in the hands of a receiver. In 1906 it was again sold, but now the bank had to line up with other creditors who wanted a piece of the sale price. It was not until late 1908 that the courts set the bank's claim at $600,000, $100,000 of which would be paid in cash with the rest to come over time. Of the remainder, only $381,000 was ever paid to the bank, and this in two payments to the liquidator, one made in 1911 and another in 1913.[25]

With its assets largely immobilized by these two large accounts the bank stumbled through its last decade of operations until the failure of the Banque de St-Jean finally led to its close. It saw its profits as a percentage of its paid capital fall from 10.5% in 1898, to 5.9% in 1903, and to 3.3% by 1907. With the decline of profits no new funds were added to the reserve, and dividends were not paid after 1903. This situation led to protests from shareholders, who believed that their investment had been squandered by Dessaulles and the other directors with ties to the railway and the city's industries. Particularly aggrieved were rural shareholders, who had held the majority of bank stock in 1874, but who owned less than one-third by 1908. Residents of the rural parishes of Rouville, Bagot, and St-Hyacinthe counties occupied four of the ten seats on the bank's first board of directors, but only one of six seats on the last. Following the bank's closure these rural shareholders showed their resentment of Dessaulles' policies by sending numerous petitions to the federal government seeking exemption from their double liability, since the bank's problems had been caused by the 'maladministration' of a small clique.[26]

Equally vocal were several of the directors who had no ties to the firms supported by the bank. Heading this group was Eusèbe Morin, a St-Hyacinthe merchant. In 1902 Morin proposed a reduction in the bank's dividend so that some bad debts might be written off the books, while in 1905 he called for the payment of another 10% of the bank's subscribed capital, but in each case he failed because his proposals were hostile to the interests of the largest shareholders.[27] Following this second failure he resigned from the board, noting that the bank was doomed as long as there was 'une opposition systématique et constante de certains directeurs, trop prompts à favoriser leurs intérêts personnels au détriment de la banque.'[28]

The directors were not prepared to reach into their own pockets to bolster the bank, but they had no reluctance to turn to the residents of the region for further funds. In its early years the Banque de St-Hyacinthe went after savings deposits in a conservative fashion, so that it had only one branch and deposits of roughly $400,000 in 1891. But as the bank found itself chronically short of ready cash it followed the lead of the other French banks and looked to the savings of francophone farmers. By 1903 the bank had established four new branches so as to bring the deposits in its vaults to $1 million on the eve of its suspension. Most successful was the branch at St-Césaire whose ledgers at the time of the suspension showed deposits of $180,000, and loans of only $40,000.[29]

By 1903, with its assets tied up in loans of dubious value and with substantial deposits on the books, the bank had degenerated to such a degree that the president of the Canadian Bankers' Association (CBA) warned Dessaulles of 'the inadequacy of the liquid assets to meet an emergency.'[30] In order to meet its serious cash-flow problem, the bank entered into an arrangement for the rediscounting of its notes with the Eastern Townships Bank, but when it lost $100,000 in deposits in the two months following the suspension of the Banque St-Jean the CBA believed that direct action had to be taken.[31] On 22 June 1908 the bank's cashier, L.F. Philie, met with John Knight, the secretary of the CBA, in Montreal to discuss the situation in St-Hyacinthe. They met once more the following day, at which time Knight came to the conclusion that 'the only honest thing to do was to recommend the Bank to suspend payment.' The two men then returned to St-Hyacinthe, and at a meeting of the directors Knight presented his recommendation. When a few of the directors balked, Knight pointed out that if the suspension were not forthcoming he 'would report to the Minister of Finance that the bank was insolvent.'[32] The directors were appropriately intimidated, and the bank closed its doors for good on 24 June.

Over the next few years the liquidation of the Banque de St-Hyacinthe proceeded peacefully under the supervision of Philie, its last cashier. The double liability of the shareholders was invoked, and the depositors were repaid in full with even a small interest payment. On the surface it appeared that the depositors had been spared another disaster thanks to the action of the CBA, but this generous interpretation was called into question by J.H. Rainville, the federal deputy from Chambly and Verchères, at parliamentary hearings for the revision of the Bank Act in 1913. Rainville contended that Knight had acted under the instructions of the president of the CBA, Edward Clouston, who was also the president of the Bank of Montreal. Clouston allegedly wanted the bank to close so that his own institution might move into St-Hyacinthe, an eventuality that came to pass within two days of the suspension. Rainville found it suspicious 'that papers, books, stamps all with the name: Bank of Montreal, St-Hyacinthe were in readiness, the very day after the Bank of St-Hyacinthe was closed. It was the wolf devouring the rabbit.'[33] Moreover, the Bank of Montreal also moved in to take over the Banque de St-Hyacinthe's most lucrative branch at St-Césaire.

As for the weak position of the bank, Rainville contended that the situation had been overblown so as to achieve the desired ends. He claimed that deposits had firmed up by June 1908, a fact that is supported by the noticeable slowing down of withdrawals during the second month after the closure in St-Jean. On the issue of deposits, Rainville could not understand why, if affairs were so desperate, substantial deposits would have been made by two of the directors only two days before the suspension.[34] Nor could he understand how Knight could have claimed that a suspension was mandatory because a crowd of depositors was forming outside the bank. According to Rainville, people who were passing by at the time remembered seeing no such crowd. In terms of additional funds that could have seen the bank through its hard times, Rainville pointed to the $173,563 of subscribed capital that had still not been called in, and there was also the Quebec Southern claim which momentarily appeared on the verge of settlement in June 1908.

In addition to his analysis of the bank's situation, Knight had allegedly also resorted to intimidation to convince the directors to close up shop, and following Rainville's disclosure of these actions the CBA did nothing in public to cast doubt upon the judgment of Knight and Clouston.[35] In private, however, the president of the association, D.P. Wilkie of the Imperial Bank, wrote as follows to the finance minister, W.T. White: 'It would appear that not only Mr. Knight but the Bank itself acted hastily and without due consideration for the interests involved, but in any event I beg to inform you that there was no consultation with the Council of the Association and Mr. Knight's course was approved of by those who are no longer in the Association.'[36] This last reference is presumably to Clouston, who Knight insisted was supportive of all of his actions.[37]

The essence of Rainville's case was that the Bank of Montreal, through Clouston, had been instrumental in the destruction of a bank that was still viable. The designs of the Bank of Montreal are not difficult to imagine, particularly in the light of its growing interest in the francophone market in the 1900s. During the first decade of the new century the bank increased the number of its Quebec branches from three to twenty-two, with nearly half of these offices situated in towns more than 75% French. Still, there were limits to its enthusiasm for the Quebec market, as was evident from its early exit from St-Césaire following its takeover of the Banque de St-Hyacinthe's office. This withdrawal was in spite of the fact that the branch offered deposits superior to the level set by the Bank of Montreal for the opening of new rural offices.[38]

As to whether the Banque de St-Hyacinthe could have successfully continued operations beyond June 1908, it is impossible to say. Rainville imagined a situation such as that whereby the Banque Jacques-Cartier successfully transformed itself following a suspension into the Banque Provinciale. Since there was never any run on the Banque de St-Hyacinthe office for deposits, it seems reasonable to assume that it might have been able to gain a delay in the repayment of depositors such as was gained by the Jacques-Cartier. In addition, the remainder of the subscribed capital of the Banque de St-Hyacinthe needed to be called in to write off some of the old debts, and then new sources of capital would have been required to resume normal operations. The Banque Jacques-Cartier was able to find new capital only because of its well-to-do supporters in Montreal and a clientele that spanned the province. Whether this would have been possible for a small-town French bank is less likely. Even if these funds had been found, the long-term future for such a small bank in the age of monopoly capitalism was an uncertain one, as the passing from the scene of the Eastern Townships Bank amply demonstrates.

IV

On the surface the Eastern Townships Bank (ETB) appeared as different from the Banque de St-Hyacinthe as any bank could have been. Throughout its history, over 99% of the shares of the Sherbrooke-based bank were held by English-speaking investors who, in turn, chose an exclusively anglophone group of men to serve as directors. Appearances aside, however, the two banks ran very similar operations during the late nineteenth century. At the time that the Banque de St-Hyacinthe was being formed, the ETB was still a small bank with a paid capital of only $400,000 in 1871, even though it had been in existence since the late 1850s. Up to the 1870s the bank's capital was largely controlled by rural interests from the Eastern Townships, on whose behalf a clause was inserted in the bank's charter denying large shareholders voting privileges proportional to their investment. In the same spirit, a by-law was adopted shortly after the bank began operations which limited the indebtedness tht could be incurred by any person or firm to $10,000.[39]

In spite of these various incentives to bring the investments of farmers to the bank, the institution was firmly under the control of the major business leaders of the region from the very start. The bank's first president, Benjamin Pomroy, was one of the original directors of the Paton Manufacturing Company, which operated the woollen mill that was Sherbrooke's most important source of employment by the early 1870s. The president of the Paton operation, R.W. Heneker, succeeded Pomroy as president of the bank in 1874, and under both of these men considerable support was extended to local industry. The bank's commitment to industrial development was reflected in its 1871 annual report, which noted that Sherbrooke might become 'the most important seat of manufactures in the Dominion outside Montreal.'[40]

Because of this link to Sherbrooke's industrial future, the bank's capital was increased to $1 million by 1875, and at Heneker's insistence the ceiling on loans was removed in the same year. Heneker's role in the Sherbrooke economy was in many ways analogous to Dessaulles' in St-Hyacinthe. While the latter's rise to prominence was linked to his family's seigneurial holdings, Heneker came to Sherbrooke as commissioner of the British American Land Company, the region's major landlord. While Dessaulles headed the Compagnie Manufacturière before becoming a bank president, Heneker came to lead the ETB following a number of years as president of the Paton firm. With this background, Heneker facilitated a $275,000 loan to Paton in 1880.[41] He also provided loans to the region's railways that amounted to $500,000 by the mid-1890s.[42]

Heneker's policy of associating the bank with industrial projects seems to have served it well throughout the first twenty years of his presidency. This is hardly surprising in light of Sherbrooke's development as an industrial centre between 1871 and 1891. The number of workers in the city increased by 170% during this period, while the population grew by 130%. Leading the way was the Paton factory, which employed 725 workers by 1892. The bank benefited from these developments, recording profits that were consistently above the norm for comparable banks, paying healthy dividends, and building up a reserve fund that reached $750,000 by 1896.

But as the 1890s progressed, Sherbrooke industry, dependent as was St-Hyacinthe's upon woollen and textile manufacturing, began to suffer from excess capacity. In 1894 *Le Prix Courant* noted, 'La manufacture de lainages de la Paton Manufacturing Company est fermée pour un temps indéterminé. La compagnie dit que c'est pour faire des réparations mais on prétend que c'est plutôt faute de commandes suffisantes.'[43] The company lost money intermittently throughout the 1890s, was employing only five hundred workers by 1900, and did not again see profits comparable to those of the 1880s until the outbreak of World War I.[44] With the slowing down of the city's industrial development the bank recorded profits well below those for comparable banks for three consecutive years beginning in 1892.

This is where the similarities between Heneker and Dessaulles and between their two banks begin to break down. Dessaulles and his allies had few connections beyond their region, so that once St-Hyacinthe industry began to decline they had no opportunity to find other good investments or new sources of capital. Heneker, by contrast, had business connections beyond the Townships that had permitted him to bring Montreal investors, most notably George Stephen, to invest in the Paton Mill.[45] Some years later the *Sherbrooke Daily Record* commented that 'Montrealers are always willing to give [Heneker] a hearing when he comes among them for any purpose.'[46] Heneker was also able to call upon the support of New Englanders who had ties to the neighbouring Townships for both geographical and genealogical reasons. Many Townshippers were able to trace their roots back to New England, and among the founders of the bank only Heneker did not have such a connection. Accordingly, as the Eastern Townships Bank increased its capital from $400,000 in 1871 to $1.5 million in 1892 most of the new capital came from Montrealers and New Englanders. While Townshippers owned 83% of ETB stock in 1871, this figure fell to 57% in 1892.

These broader connections made no difference to bank policy

until the 1890s since business in the Townships had produced sound profits. In fact, up to the mid-1890s all of the bank's branches were situated in the region. But when the bank's profitability began to slip these connections provided both the incentive and the means for it to break out of its narrow role. In 1899, for instance, the bank established its first branch beyond Quebec. S.H.C. Miner, a long-time client and future director of the bank, was about to establish a smelter at Grand Forks, British Columbia, and he advised Heneker in advance of any public announcement so that the ETB might be 'the first in the field.' Miner assured the bank that 'it would receive the business of the smelting company and the mines with which he was connected.'[47] By 1902 advances to Miner's smelter reached $250,000.[48] But this was only the start of the bank's transformation from a regional into a national institution. Still further capital was raised until the $3 million mark was reached in 1907, the majority of which was now held by people residing outside the region. As for the board of directors, it did not have a single member from outside the Townships before 1894, but barely had a majority of Townshippers by 1912. Accordingly, the bank's branches outside the area multiplied, particularly under its new president, William Farwell, who succeeded Heneker in 1902. Branches were established in French regions of Quebec that had earlier been shunned, but more significant was the one branch located in Montreal and the eleven situated outside the province in 1911. In 1909 these branches, which accounted for only 15% of all the bank's offices, were responsible for nearly 40% of all credit extended by the ETB.[49]

By 1911 the Eastern Townships Bank was a national, and not merely a regional, institution. The policy of expansion to generate deposits that began in the mid-1890s was so successful that in 1911 savings deposits represented 54% of total liabilities, the second-highest percentage recorded by a Quebec bank. There were also other signs of success in the bank's affairs during the first decade of the new century as dividends never fell below 8%, net profits continually exceeded 12% of paid capital, and the reserve fund grew until it reached $2.4 million by 1911. The dividends that were paid were generally superior to those paid by comparable banks, but the profits, impressive as they might have appeared at first glance, were less than those recorded by comparable banks in eight of the bank's last nine years of operations. It was not that the bank's affairs were unprofitable but rather that they were less profitable than those of institutions with head offices in Canada's major centres and with easy access to information and clients. In order to resolve this problem, the directors seriously considered moving the head office to Montreal in 1911.[50]

The move to Montreal was precluded, however, by the acquisition of the bank by the Bank of Commerce, which took place in 1912. The offer to purchase, made late in 1911, was received just as a group of directors returned from a trip to the West to look into affairs in that part of the country. The directors found that they needed to establish numerous new branches in the West if they hoped to retain their share of the market in the face of fierce competition from the larger banks. New capital would have to be found just for the bank to hold its own by opening new branches, and directors who already saw net profits as a percentage of paid capital running behind those of comparable banks had to wonder if the expansion was worth the effort. Particularly dubious were the directors who resided outside of the region and who represented the majority of shareholders by 1911. For them there was no emotional attachment involved in preserving the bank. When the Bank of Montreal offered to acquire the Eastern Townships Bank in 1905, the proposal was rejected as profits were still acceptable, but following years of relatively weak profits the leaders from outside the region became the most enthusiastic supporters of the proposition by the Commerce.[51] In fact, the only opposition to the deal came from two directors from the Townships.[52] But while the only opposition to the merger came from local interests, the majority of directors from the region recognized the offer made by the Commerce as a sound one which they gladly accepted. With the exchange in 1912 of the $3 million of Eastern Townships Bank stock for $3 million of Bank of Commerce shares, what was then the largest bank acquisition yet seen in Canada was completed.

v

The 'logic' of the policy pursued by the Eastern Townships Bank beginning in the 1890s ultimately led to its passing from the scene. While some investors from the region may have mourned the loss of a bank they could call their own, they at least gained a profit on their investment, while the shareholders in the Banque de St-Hyacinthe saw their capital disappear along with the bank. However, the type of policy pursued by the ETB was never an option for a small-town French bank. Even the larger French banks of Montreal and Quebec City had to await the emergence of a significant pool of savings across the province before they were able to expand in the 1880s and 1890s. None of them had been able to establish themselves in English communities outside Quebec, nor for that matter had they shown an ability to secure the accounts of important English clients within the province. For a bank such as the Banque de St-Hyacinthe, whose affairs were further restricted to the French population of its region, there was no escape from the problems that emerged in 1890s. While three of the French banks of Montreal and Quebec City survived well into the next century, there was really no future for the small-town French banks, which were doubly cursed by being both small and French.

5

The Survivors: 1900–1921

I

As the new century began, all but three of the French banks of Montreal and Quebec City had passed from the scene, and the small-town banks were entering their last years. The Banque d'Hochelaga, the Banque Nationale, and the Banque Provinciale were the survivors, and through the first two decades of the 1900s they operated without the recurring crises that marked French banking in the nineteenth century. This was a period of con-solidation within the Canadian banking industry, with twenty-one chartered banks disappearing by means of mergers, but the designs of the large English banks never included these French institutions. Nor for that matter did the English banks threaten the hold of the French institutions upon the francophone Quebec market through the expansion of their branch systems. The num-ber of branches situated in Quebec by the English banks in-creased during this period, but most continued to be located in Montreal or in towns across the province with relatively weak French populations.[1] As a result, the French banks had to face their English counterparts head-on in relatively few spots across Quebec. Abbé Groulx claimed in 1921 that the English banks were going 'jusqu'au fond de nos campagnes à drainer l'argent des petits épargnistes,' but there is little evidence to justify his concern.[2]

With the English banks largely removed from the picture, the three French institutions moved in to drain off the savings that francophone Quebecers had at their disposal during a period of significant economic change in the province. Between 1901 and 1921 the value of agricultural production in Quebec increased by more than twice the rate in Ontario, new natural resources came into play, and the value of industrial production in current dollars more than doubled.[3] Feeding off these developments, the paid capital of the three French banks increased from $3.6 million in 1901 to nearly $9 million in 1921, with 95% of the new funds coming from francophone Quebecers. In addition, these banks increased their deposits by 1100%, twice the figure for the industry as a whole, by bringing their number of branches in the province to 365 by 1921, a far cry from the 40 which they were operating in 1901. The only threat which the French branches could see to their lock on these savings was the establishment of over one hundred caisses populaires, but this challenge was adequately met through the opening of another 365 subagencies across the province.

In fact, the most serious competition for the savings of francophone Quebecers was waged among the three banks. None of them indicated any great success during this period in penetrating English markets outside the province, so that each jealously guarded its position within Quebec. Typical was the situation in the early 1920s at Rivière-du-Loup when the Nationale hired the Provinciale's manager to head its own branch in the town. Joseph Pratte was given a $1,000 raise and apparently went door to door trying to lure clients from one bank to the other.[4] In retaliation, the Provinciale hired the accountant of the Nationale's branch at Montmagny to manage its new branch there.[5] The Canadian Bankers' Association was eventually brought in to try to settle the dispute. This was not the first time that it had tried to curb the competition between the French banks. During World War 1 its committee on branches had drawn up a set of guidelines to limit the opening of new offices, because of the unavailability of manpower, but these guidelines never came into effect because five banks, including the three French institutions, opposed it.[6] Later in the war the CBA tried to get the banks at least to justify their opening of new offices, but the Nationale would not even respond to the request while the Provinciale reserved for itself the right to act 'when[ever] its territory was invaded.'[7]

The three French banks may have operated with funds gained from a single pool of savings, but the way in which these monies were invested varied greatly from bank to bank. These differing strategies reflected the histories of the three institutions prior to 1900 and the connections and interests of their leaders. The Banque Provinciale's affairs, for instance, were deeply influenced by its earlier history as the Banque Jacques-Cartier. Eager to assure depositors that their funds would be safely invested, the Provinciale became heavily involved in dealing in stocks and bonds. By contrast, the Banque d'Hochelaga had developed close ties with the English-speaking business establishment of Montreal in the late 1800s, and its securing of some major industrial accounts in the new century reflected these connections. As for the Banque Nationale, it never really expanded beyond the stage of an institution with close ties to the business of its region, and the bank's affairs between 1900 and 1921 reflected this orientation.

All three of these strategies provided profits during this period, with the result that, if one controls for the size of the bank, the French institutions were more profitable than their English counterparts.[8] With their access to funds and with the profitability of their operations, the assets of the three banks grew by 840% as opposed to 490% for the industry as a whole. Between 1900 and 1921 the French banks secured for themselves a lasting place within Canadian banking.

II

Of the three French banks, the Banque Provinciale experienced the greatest growth during this period. By 1921 both the Hochelaga and the Nationale had assets of roughly $75 million, while the Provinciale's figure was only $44 million. Nevertheless, the latter bank's assets had increased by nearly 1400% during the two previous decades while neither of the other two could show an increase of over 1000%. Both the Nationale and the Hochelaga entered the new century in good shape. Neither had had to repay large numbers of depositors during the panic of 1899, and both had earned solid profits during the 1890s. By contrast, the Banque Provinciale did not even exist as the new century began. Its predecessor, the Banque Jacques-Cartier, experienced its second suspension in 1899 and was just about to reduce its capital for the third time as the 1900s began. The Provinciale only came into existence in July 1900, and by the start of the following year still had assets of less than $3 million. Accordingly, the bank had a long way to go to reach its 1921 position.

The Provinciale, led by its general manager, Tancrède Bienvenu, carefully looked for ways to grow by attracting the savings of francophone Quebecers. The bank pledged that all savings of less than $1,000 would be secured by investments in stocks and bonds or in call loans guaranteed by such paper. In addition, a board of commissioners (*commissaires-censeurs*), separate from the board of directors, was to be established to assure that this commitment, which was later extended to include all savings deposits, was honoured.[9] This was an early form of deposit insurance, and it apparently struck a responsive chord among francophone Quebecers whose savings had taken a beating during the 1890s, not only because of the troubles of the Banque Jacques-Cartier but also through the failures of the Banque du Peuple and the Ville-Marie. Within two months of the launching of the Provinciale, Bienvenu could announce to the directors that he had received requests from towns seeking branches which would have 'le bénéfice du département d'épargnes contrôlé par les Commissaires-Censeurs.'[10]

By 1921 the bank had over $30 million in deposits, which represented 66% of its total liabilities, the highest figure recorded in that year by a Quebec-based institution. That these savings were drawn from a largely francophone market is evident from the location of the Provinciale's branches. While it inherited only six offices from the Jacques-Cartier, there were 158 by 1921, three-quarters of which were located in Quebec. The vast majority of these offices were situated in towns with populations that were more than 75% French. In this spirit the bank established a branch at Danville in the Eastern Townships because 'over 50% of the population [was] of the French language and there [was] as yet no French Canadian bank represented.'[11] A similar sort of logic operated in the establishment of the bank's branches in Ontario and the Maritimes. The eastern branches were aimed exclusively at the Acadian population, with the result that the Provinciale was fond of referring to itself as the 'Banque des Acadiens.' As for its Ontario operations, typical was its opening of a branch at Tilbury because of 'the special request of the French population.'[12] The bank even considered the opening of branches in a number of New England towns with significant Franco-American populations. New Bedford, Lowell, and Worcester were seen as good sites because their populations were 'composed of a great number of French Canadians from whom the bank [could] reasonably expect encouragement.'[13] But in spite of the directors' resolve upon several occasions to open at New Bedford, no concrete action was ever taken.[14]

In honouring its commitments regarding the investment of the savings deposits gained through these branches, the Banque Provinciale's assets came to be distributed in a distinctive fashion. By 1921 nearly half of the bank's funds were tied up in call loans or in stocks and bonds, and with 20% of its assets in the first category and 27% in the second it led all Quebec banks. This orientation provided the bank with what the directors described as 'opérations qui sont plus sûres mais qui donnent des profits moins élevés que les prêts au commerce.'[15] Nevertheless, the bank consistently earned profits that were above the norm for Quebec institutions of its size, and through the issuing of modest dividends it was able to build up a reserve fund of $1.3 million by 1921.

This involvement in the world of stocks and bonds took the Provinciale in a unique direction. Not only did the other French banks invest a relatively small percentage of their assets in these securities, but when they did make such investments they tended to be in federal, provincial, or municipal securities which were

TABLE 5.1
Selected assets of the French banks, January 1921

	% of total assets		% of securities		
	Call loans	Securities	Federal & provincial	Municipal & foreign	Railway & other bonds
Provinciale	20	27	22	57	21
Nationale	6	19	37	56	7
Hochelaga	6	11	28	70	2

Source: See appendix 1.

comparatively safe and about which little specialized knowledge was required. The Provinciale, by contrast, invested heavily in railway, public utility, and industrial stocks and bonds with which francophone bankers such as Bienvenu had historically had little familiarity. In 1921, 20% of the value of the securities held by the bank came from such investments, and only the Royal Bank had a higher percentage among Quebec-based institutions. With investments of over $100,000 in the bonds of such firms as Ottawa Light, Heat and Power, Dominion Iron and Steel, and Maple Leaf Milling, the Provinciale's portfolio took it into areas that were not normally the domain of the French banks.[16]

Bienvenu was undoubtedly assisted in the management of these securities by the presence on the board of directors of Rodolphe Forget, whose brokerage firm received substantial call loans from the bank.[17] However, Forget was only on the board from 1907 to 1910, when he left to start up the short-lived Banque Internationale. More significant assistance came from a group of English-speaking directors who sat on the board from the Provinciale's beginning. In the nineteenth century the anglophones who helped in the running of the French banks tended to be marginal members of the English business community, but the men who were associated with the Provinciale had impeccable credentials. They were sought out by the bank for their expertise, and they were at the same time drawn to a French bank that intended to deal with more than the internal commerce of the province.

The first of the English directors was G.B. Burland, who took his seat on the same day that the Banque Jacques-Cartier passed out of existence. As president of the British American Bank Note Company, Burland stood to be well versed in the intricacies of banking across Canada, since his firm produced the notes used by Canada's banks under the supervision of the CBA. He was joined in 1902 by the prominent Montreal merchant and manufacturer Samuel Carsley, and throughout the next quarter-century there would always be two English-speaking directors, one of whom would serve as the bank's vice-president. In 1904 the bank's annual meeting paid tribute to Burland and Carsley, 'dont haute respectabilité et grande fortune ... ajoutent au crédit de la Banque.'[18] Carsley gave way to his son in 1909, but more significant was Burland's replacement by G.M. Bosworth, vice-president of the CPR, in 1907. The role that Bosworth could play in the bank's affairs beyond francophone Quebec was noted by its president Hormisdas Laporte in 1909: 'Owing to the potent influence of one of our directors, G.M. Bosworth, Vice-President of the CPR Company, the recent voyage to Europe of our general manager was most fortunate in its results for the bank. Without entering into the details of the exceptionally advantageous arrangements concluded with very strong European banks, we may state that the Provincial Bank is now in a position to accept the accounts of the principal commercial and industrial houses in the province, seeing that it can now have "on demand" all the necessary funds and at a rate defying competition in the market.'[19]

The management of the bank gave great weight to the advice provided by these English directors. This was the case, for instance, when it was decided not to increase the bank's subscribed capital in 1906 only after receiving letters to that effect from both Burland and Carsley, who were out of the country.[20] Deference to these men was also evident in the bank's recording its minutes intermittently in English and in its request in 1906 to have its charter amended so that it might operate with the English translation of its name. This last action led some to wonder if the Provinciale was still a French bank, but such concerns were unfounded.[21] While the English directors particularly provided advice related to the bank's place in larger capital markets, they exercised little or no influence over the bank's everyday operations relating to the collecting of deposits and the granting of commercial loans. Burland, Bosworth, and the Carsleys were among the bank's largest shareholders, but few other English-speakers held Provinciale stocks. Between 1901 and 1921 the bank's capital increased from $862,000 to $3 million, and over 90% of these funds came from francophone investors. The most important of these investors were the French-speaking business-men who monopolized the majority of the seats on the board of directors. They provided the direction for the bank to establish most of its branches in French communities, and it was their instructions that led the manager of the branch at Papineauville to write the following letter to local residents who were dealing with the Union Bank: A titre de représentant d'une institution cana-dienne-française je viens solliciter l'ouverture de votre compte de dépôts à la Banque Provinciale à Papineauville. Sans doute, je comprends qu'il y a plusieurs années que vous faites vos affaires de Banque à la Banque Union, mais aujourd'hui vous avez l'avan-tage d'avoir une institution canadienne-française dans votre loca-lité, pourquoi ne pas lui donner la préférence à une institution anglaise?'[22]

These same men also extended to francophones over 90% of the credit provided to the bank's most important clients.[23] In 1923 one-quarter of the value of the bank's current loans was tied up in the accounts of those borrowers who owed over $100,000, and prominent among those clients were several of the directors. Hormisdas Laporte, of the important wholesale grocery firm of Laporte, Martin et Compagnie, was the president of the bank from 1907 to 1934. Laporte, Martin owed the bank $275,000 in 1923, and another $107,000 was owed by the Librairie Beauche-min, of which the long-term director L.J.O. Beauchemin was the president.[24] When Beauchemin left the board in 1922 he was replaced by the bookstore's vice-president, Emilien Daoust. The

Banque Provinciale evolved as a partnership between these francophone businessmen and their English colleagues. The former
directed the bank to establish its branches in French communities
and to support French commerce through the granting of short-
term credit, while the latter attended to the investment of the
savings deposits in the capital market.

III

The Banque d'Hochelaga entered the new century as the French
bank best loved by the English business community, and nothing
that happened over the next twenty years weakened these ties.
English shareholders did not play an important part in the
Hochelaga's affairs. In fact, nearly all of the additional funds that
were raised to take its capital from $1.5 to $4 million came from
francophones. Moreover, English-speakers never wielded great
influence on the Hochelaga's board of directors. There was one
seat on the board that was reserved for an anglophone, but none
of its occupants were treated with the sort of deference evident in
the affairs of the Banque Provinciale.[25] Rather, the ties of the
Hochelaga to Montreal's English business elite were cemented by
several of its French-speaking directors, most notably Joseph-
Marcellin Wilson and F.L. Béïque. Wilson was a director from
1906 to the changing of the bank's name in 1925, while Béïque
joined him from 1910 to 1925. Wilson reached the board from his
position as head of Boivin, Wilson and Company, owners of the
Melchers' Distillery, whose account he brought to the bank in
return for his seat.[26] He also brought along his connections with
Herbert Holt from his position on the board of Montreal Light,
Heat and Power, and he was among the first francophones to sit
on the board of the CPR.

In this last capacity Wilson was joined by the lawyer Béïque,
whose clients read like a Who's Who of the elite of Canadian
business. He was involved with Herbert Holt in enterprises such
as North Star Mining and the Calgary and Edmonton Railway,
but his real claim to notoriety was his position as lawyer and
lobbyist for the leaders of the cotton industry, most notably A.F.

Gault and David Morrice.[27] In 1897 these two men used Béïque as their lobbyist to gain tariff concessions from the federal government, and in the early 1900s they employed him once again, this time to bring about the merger of Dominion Cotton Mills, Merchants' Cotton Company, Montmorency Cotton, and Colonial Bleaching and Printing into Dominion Textiles. For his services to Gault and Morrice, Béïque was ultimately rewarded with a seat on another one of their firms, Canadian Coloured Cotton. His influence in these circles was further attested to by Morrice when he wrote to Béïque, 'One of the great troubles with me is that I always do just as you want.'[28]

Within the bank Béïque quickly gained considerable influence. He was made vice-president in 1912, was instrumental in the appointment of his son-in-law Beaudry Leman as general manager in 1914, and became president of the Banque Canadienne Nationale in 1928. Béïque used this influence to involve the bank with a number of major industrial firms, several of which were operated by English-speaking interests. Among customers with advances of over $100,000, the Banque Provinciale provided the vast bulk of its credit to French-run firms. By contrast, among the Hochelaga's leading clients over one-third of the bank's advances in 1921 went to English-dominated companies. Moreover, 80% of the money advanced to these firms by the Hochelaga went to manufacturers.[29] Accordingly, the leading client in the course of 1921 was the Wayagamack Pulp and Paper Company of Trois-Rivières, which returned to the bank upon three occasions for advances that totalled nearly $3 million. Wayagamack was headed by C.R. Whitehead, with whom Béïque had considerable dealings when the former was general manager of Montmorency Cotton. Now Whitehead and Béïque were able to collaborate once more through the granting of credit not only to Wayagamack but also to Wabasso Cotton and Shawinigan Cotton. These last two firms secured advances of over $1.25 million in the course of 1921, with another $700,000 going to the Regent Securities Company guaranteed by stock in the various Whitehead firms.

In striking contrast to the bank's leading English clients, the bulk of advances to its major French borrowers went to support commercial activity. The Hochelaga's leading French client in

TABLE 5.2
Advances of over $100,000 by sector

	Banque Provinciale (1923)	Banque d'Hochelaga (1921)
Government and religious orders	24	28
Manufacturing	19	38
Commerce	46	19
Finance	–	7
Miscellaneous	11	8

Source: BNC, Banque d'Hochelaga, directors' loan decisions, 1921; PAC, RG19, vol. 817.

1921 was the dry goods firm of P.P. Martin et Compagnie with total advances of over $2.5 million, but not far behind was the Chicoutimi Pulp Company, whose figure for 1921 was nearly $2.1 million. This last firm had long been operated by J.E.A. Dubuc, but when further capital was required to continue operations it was taken over, along with other pulp and paper firms in the Saguenay – Lac St-Jean region, by the Saguenay Pulp and Power Company. The president of this firm was none other than Béïque, who was joined on the board by J.M. Wilson.

The bank was also active in the support of various industrial firms with which its leaders appeared to have no direct connection. Among the forest-related industries there were considerable advances made to the Belgo-Canadian Pulp and Paper Company and to the Three Rivers Lumber Company. Close behind these industries in the Hochelaga's operations were various boot and shoe manufacturers such as the Regina Shoe Company and the firm of Aird and Son. In all, the boot and shoe industry gained over $3.25 million in advances from the bank in the course of 1921. While the Provinciale invested heavily in stocks and bonds and provided short-term loans largely for the support of commercial activity, the Hochelaga deeply involved itself in the day-to-day affairs of industry, and during the first two decades of the century these investments allowed the bank to earn solid profits.

While a significant percentage of the Hochelaga's advances

went to English-run firms, the bulk of the savings that financed these loans came from francophones. As was the case with the other French banks, the Hochelaga greatly expanded its system of branches during this period. The bank operated only 13 branches in 1901, but the figure reached 202 by 1921. 70% of these branches were located in Quebec, and these offices brought in 85% of the bank's $55 million in total deposits by 1921. Outside Montreal the Hochelaga's Quebec offices were concentrated in small communities with overwhelmingly French populations, and the transferring of funds from the depositors of these towns to the bank's large corporate clients made the bank an easy target for those who wanted to see the expansion of the caisse populaire system.

Theoretically, each caisse was organized so that the funds that it raised in a parish would be reinvested there. As a result, Beaudry Leman was not greeted warmly when he appeared in 1922 before a committee of the Quebec Legislative Assembly that was looking into ways to expand agricultural credit through the caisses. He was asked about a hypothetical parish in which deposits from farmers equalled $75,000 but loans to the lumber industry came to $100,000. Such a situation, one deputy noted, permits you to say that the amount of deposits does not exceed that of the loans. You are right, but it is nevertheless money loaned by [and not to] farmers.'[30] Nor was there anything particularly hypothetical about this scenario: the bank's branches in the St-Maurice Valley recorded a surplus of loans over deposits of nearly $3 million in 1921. Most of the $2.6 million in deposits came from small savers, but nearly all of the $5.6 million in loans went to large industrial firms, most notably to Whitehead's various ventures in the region.[31]

In mobilizing the savings of francophone Quebecers and investing these funds far from their place of origin, the Hochelaga did nothing that was novel. The Provinciale placed its funds in securities, while the Hochelaga provided support to industry. But the Hochelaga did distinguish itself once again by refusing to be content with the savings of francophones. By 1921 both the Hochelaga and the Provinciale had roughly 30% of their branches situated outside the province, but while the latter bank did not dare venture beyond French communities, the former tried to break new ground. In 1921 the Hochelaga was the only French bank with branches on the prairies, and roughly half of the thirty-six towns where it had offices had French communities that accounted for less than 25% of the local population. In these communities, the bank had to go after the savings of English-speaking residents to succeed.

There is little evidence, however, that the Hochelaga's prairie gambit succeeded as fully one-third of its branches closed between 1921 and 1925. No matter how minimal the French population may have been in these towns, the bank had to depend upon them for support because the English residents appeared ill disposed to leave their savings with a French bank. This was the story that was conveyed by inspectors who visited these branches before they were closed. Regarding the bank's operations at Humboldt, Saskatchewan, the inspector wrote that 'la population de la ville est d'environ 2000 âmes, composée en majorité d'anglais, la balance sont des allemands.' He suggested a change in manager, but given the demographic situation he doubted there would be 'plus de succès à l'avenir que nous en avons eu par le passé.'[32] The population was similarly distributed at Laflèche, Saskatchewan, where the bank's operations were described as 'un insuccès complet.' While the English residents of Laflèche took the bulk of the advances made by the bank, nearly all of the deposits came from francophones.[33] This situation seemed to assure that loans would perpetually outstrip deposits, and the branch was closed.

With the failure of its foray into the West, the Hochelaga remained a bank whose financing, both in terms of its capital and its savings deposits, came principally from francophone Quebecers. Upon this relatively slim base, the bank set off to support firms whose capital was many times that of its own. As long as these companies, particularly those tied to the pulp and paper industry, expanded and profited, so too did the bank, but when several of the Hochelaga's clients began to falter in the 1920s the bank suffered as well.

IV

While both the Provinciale and the Hochelaga tried to move in new directions, the operations of the Banque Nationale differed very little from those of the French banks of the nineteenth century. Nor is this particularly surprising when one looks at the men who led the Nationale during the first decades of the 1900s. The board of directors barely changed across this period, led by Rodolphe Audette, who served as president from 1895 to 1921. Audette was a Quebec City merchant of modest means and limited business connections, and he was joined by other directors with similar backgrounds. While roughly 40% of the directors of the Hochelaga and the Provinciale during this period could be described as either manufacturers or financiers, the percentage was only 12% for the Nationale. Accordingly, the Nationale's leadership was not as equipped to look for new options as were the directors of the other two banks, but this is perhaps not surprising for a bank based in Quebec City, a centre whose place within the Canadian economy had long been marginal. With the increasing concentration of economic power at Montreal and Toronto, there was little incentive for major players in the economy to remain at Quebec, with the result that both of the English banks left the city during the 1910s. The Quebec Bank moved its general manager to Montreal in 1912 before its acquisition by the Royal Bank in 1917, while the Union Bank moved its head office to Winnipeg in 1912. The Nationale would be the last chartered bank with its head office at Quebec City.

As a bank with limited horizons, the Banque Nationale financed its operations from the savings of francophone Quebecers, and more particularly from the pockets of those living in the Quebec City area. In terms of the capital of the bank, which increased from $1.2 million in 1901 to $2 million in 1921, 98% of the new funds came from francophones, and 90% came from residents of the eastern half of the province. As for the bank's branches, which numbered 112 by 1921, all but three were situated in Quebec, and two-thirds of the offices in the province were located east of Trois-Rivières. Through these offices the Nationale greatly expanded its note circulation and collected substantial deposits in a manner reminiscent of the Banque du Peuple.

The Nationale increased its note circulation by means of the 1913 revision of the Bank Act, which permitted banks to deposit Dominion Notes in the federal government's Central Gold Reserve, with each dollar deposited giving it the right to circulate a dollar of notes in excess of its paid capital. In 1914 the federal government further widened the scope for expanding the note circulation by accepting the deposit of securities with the minister of finance in exchange for Dominion Notes. The latter could then be used to secure the right to issue additional bank notes. No bank took advantage of these provisions as did the Nationale, whose note circulation stood at 270% of its paid capital in 1921 as opposed to 160% for the industry as a whole.

The bank also energetically worked to collect deposits from a part of the province that was far from the most prosperous. At the start of 1921 its total deposits exceeded $46 million, roughly the same amount that the Hochelaga had gained in Quebec from its offices that were concentrated in and around Montreal. The bank's task was hardly facilitated by the intense competition that it received in the region from the caisses populaires. Desjardins' movement began at Lévis, across the St Lawrence from Quebec City, and in 1921 the majority of caisses were concentrated in the area to the east of Trois-Rivières. Accordingly, the Banque Nationale competed head-on against the caisses in more towns than did the other two French banks combined. But a caisse populaire simply in the vicinity of a Banque Nationale branch could also drain off deposits. Accordingly, the bank's manager at Montmagny wrote to the head office in 1915 that he was losing deposits to the caisse at nearby St-Paul du Buton.[34]

Napoléon Lavoie, the general manager of the bank from 1910 to 1922, responded to this threat through both covert and overt activities. The former amounted to a veritable campaign of dirty tricks as Lavoie instructed managers to spread rumours regarding the instability of the caisses. He wrote to one of his managers: 'Sans faire bruit, et discrètement, quand vous apprendrez que l'on veut implanter une de ces caisses chez-vous ou dans les

paroisses où vous êtes intéressé, dites aux gens que vous connais-
sez que ces caisses, au lieu d'être avantageuses pour eux, leur
sont nuisibles.'[35] The overt activities of the Nationale consisted of
the opening of 211 subagencies by 1921, more than the number
operated by the Hochelaga and the Provinciale together. Since
the Nationale was primarily concerned with the deposits that
might be lost to the caisses, these subagencies, which could not
extend any credit, provided a simple means of competing with
Desjardins. So successful were the subagencies that they were
responsible for bringing in over one-quarter of the Nationale's
total deposits in April 1924.[36] This amounted to $10 million that
might otherwise have gone to the caisses. Accordingly, Desjardins claimed that 'la Banque Nationale nous persécute partout ...
Elle cherche à écraser les Caisses en ouvrant des sous-agences
partout où il y a des caisses. La Banque Nationale nous fait la
guerre la plus mesquine possible.'[37] For his part, Lavoie, who
was described by Desjardins as 'un prétentieux bouffi d'orgeuil,'
simply noted that the subagencies had made the bank 'more
closely connected with the rural classes than ever' and had precluded the need for such a 'European system' as the caisses.[38]

Through its note circulation and the securing of substantial
deposits, the Banque Nationale's total assets at the start of 1921
were greater than those of the other two French banks, even if its
paid capital was considerably less. By doing a large business on a
relatively small capital, the bank earned solid profits during most
of this period, with net profits as a percentage of paid capital
exceeding 25% in 1919, 1920, and 1921. During those years only
the Royal Bank, among Quebec-based institutions, came even
close to rivalling the profits recorded by the Nationale. But, as
had been the case with the French banks in the nineteenth century, a bank such as the Nationale could only earn these profits by
lending out its funds as quickly as they came in. The Nationale
rarely invested funds in call loans or in stocks and bonds, with the
result that its liquidity ratio at the start of 1921 was less than
10%.[39] By contrast, the Hochelaga's figure stood at 14% and the
Provinciale's, not surprisingly, at 32%. The situation was not
dangerous to the Nationale as long as its investments were sound

and its depositors did not require their funds back at the same time.

Such a demand by depositors was a distinct possibility, even though the bulk of deposits held by the Nationale were in savings accounts from which withdrawals could technically be made only upon the giving of fifteen days' notice. In practice, however, depositors could retrieve their funds simply by sacrificing a few weeks' interest.[40] Accordingly, from the bank's point of view all deposits, whether in current or savings accounts, might be withdrawn at any moment, and some of the Nationale's own internal records indicate that no distinctions were made between the two types of accounts.[41] For the Banque Nationale, and to a lesser degree for the Banque d'Hochelaga, there was the risk that the collapse of a major client could trigger a chain reaction that might bring down the bank, and given the Nationale's experience during this period with its largest account, the danger of such a collapse was real.

The Nationale's most important client by 1921 was the Montmagny-based Machine Agricole Nationale Limitée, whose history can be traced back to 1902. At that time Montmagny, situated on the south shore of the St Lawrence twenty-five miles east of Lévis, was a town of less than 2,000 residents that functioned as a service centre for the region. The opening of the Compagnie Manufacturière de Montmagny was seen as an event that might change the face of the town. The firm had an authorized capital of $40,000 and was prepared to produce machinery of all kinds, but few of the hopes for the company were realized in its first decade. No dividends were paid during its first ten years, and in 1908 its directors decided that it was 'impossible de continuer les opérations de cette compagnie. Il faut essayer de trouver un ou plusieurs acheteurs qui possèdent les capitaux suffisants pour continuer les opérations.'[42] No takers were forthcoming, and the company continued to struggle along until 1911 when it began to produce road-building equipment for a Quebec City firm run by Charles Paquet. A stalwart of the provincial Liberal party and later a Liberal member of the Legislative Assembly, Paquet was easily able to gain government contracts for machinery which he then passed on to Montmagny. The Compagnie Manufacturière was to build eighty machines for Paquet in 1911, but the size of the order forced it to look for additional financing. An advance of $65,000 was secured from the Banque Nationale, thus beginning a long and not always happy relationship.[43]

One could hardly foresee the problems to come from the enthusiasm of the bank's Montmagny manager in a letter written to Lavoie in 1913, 'La compagnie a fait les affaires d'or durant cette période de temps. Il y a deux ans les bâtisses couvraient une superficie de 7876 pieds carrés: elles en couvrent à présent 28,550. En 1910, elle employait en moyenne 35 hommes, maintenant c'est une moyenne de 140 hommes qui y travaillent à l'année.'[44] Further growth was promised by the sale later in the year of the Compagnie Manufacturière to the firm of Usines Générales de Chars et de Machineries in which Paquet was the leading force.[45] The new company had an authorized capital of $500,000, which was later increased to $1 million. In addition, it received a $25,000 bonus from the city of Montmagny in return for which it was to build new machinery valued at $100,000 and to employ 250 workers. Paquet's visions of grandeur also extended to the building of a small city for his workers on excess land that he had acquired, and in 1916 he set up the Société de Construction de Montmagny towards this end.

The Banque Nationale's involvement with Paquet's firm remained on a relatively modest scale up to the start of World War I, but with the availability of lucrative defence contracts Paquet transformed his factory into a munitions plant with the support of the bank to the tune of $2 million by the start of 1917. Paquet entered into various contracts with the Imperial Munitions Board in the course of 1916, few of which were completed by the start of the following year.[46] Accordingly, Lavoie wrote to Paquet, 'Le crédit accordé a dépassé de trois fois le montant demandé. Les usines, qui devaient être prêts en août ou septembre [1916], ne le sont pas encore et votre contrat d'obus, qui devait être terminé au 31 décembre [1916], ne fait que commencer. Donc faillite sur toute la ligne.' To make matters worse, Lavoie chronicled an administration that was both 'extravagante et malhonnête.' Paquet provided himself with a salary of $150 per week together with a bonus for each shell produced, and took another $11,000 of company funds with no justification whatsoever.[47]

As the war came to an end Paquet's relations with the bank improved. With the completion of his factory, orders worth over $3 million were filled during 1918, and his debt to the bank was reduced to $700,000. Looking back on this time in the company's history, Lavoie was much more charitable than he had been in 1917. 'Son actif était le double de sa dette. Elle avait prouvé ses capacités à travers bien des difficultés et la compétence de son organisation à entreprendre de grands travaux.'[48] In spite of these improvements in Paquet's operation one would have thought that the bank had had enough to do with him, but this was not the case. With the end of the war Paquet wanted to transform the Montmagny plant into a factory for the production of farm machinery, and towards this end he changed the firm's name to Machine Agricole Nationale Limitée in 1919. The new company had an authorized capital of $4 million, and it gained further financing by issuing $2 million in bonds and through advances from the bank that reached at least $2.3 million by the start of 1921.[49] Nor was this the bank's only large outstanding account, as it was owed $1.25 million by the Transportation and Shipping Company of Quebec City, a firm whose authorized capital was only $48,000.[50]

Because of the bank's financial structure it could not afford to let these firms collapse: the news of such an event would lead to a run by depositors who would find their money unavailable. In the early months of 1921 Paquet's seemingly insatiable appetite for further credit absorbed an additional $1.5 million in bank funds, all of which came from the increase in total deposits from $46 million to $50 million during the first four months of the year.[51] In addition, the bank aided Paquet by selling a new issue of Machine Agricole bonds through its branches.

Lavoie would later comment that 'la position de la banque était magnifique' in May 1921, and on the surface this assessment seemed reasonable.[52] At the start of June the shareholders were gratified by the payment of an unprecedented dividend of 12%, for the bank had earned net profits that exceeded 25% of its paid capital for the third year in a row. But just beneath the surface there was the danger that the slightest crisis could lead to a demand by depositors for funds that could not be repaid. Lavoie had been a banker since 1875 and was an employee of the Banque du Peuple at the time of its collapse in 1895. Perhaps he remembered that that bank had also tabled a rosy report only a few months before its demise.

v

Some difficult times lay ahead for the Banque d'Hochelaga and, more particularly, for the Banque Nationale. Nevertheless, at the start of 1921 the leaders of the three French banks could look back on two decades of solid growth and sound profits, and this performance was financed almost exclusively out of the savings of francophone Quebecers. While there was little change in the place of savings deposits as a percentage of total liabilities for the industry as a whole between 1901 and 1921, the figure for the French banks increased from 40% to 59%.[53] This was partly a function of the increased importance of deposits among the smaller banks in general, but even among banks of their own size the French institutions still stood out.[54]

The French banks took hold of these savings in spite of the more visible presence of the English banks in the province and the very real competition provided by the caisses populaires. The leaders of these banks, and particularly those who directed the Hochelaga and the Provinciale, were sufficiently impressed by the savings available in the province that they also involved themselves in the operation of other types of financial intermediaries during the period. Among Quebec's trust companies, the Société d'Administration Générale was established in 1902, while Trust Général was formed in 1909. Five of the directors of the Banque Provinciale were also sitting on the board of the former firm in 1913, while the Hochelaga's F.L. Béïque was the founder of the latter.[55] In terms of the life insurance industry, the Provin-

TABLE 5.3
Savings deposits as a percentage of total liabilities: Quebec banks, 1919

Total assets	%
$10–25 million (all French)	55
$25–100 million	44
English	38
French	49
+$100 million (all English)	33

Source: See appendix I.

ciale's Hormisdas Laporte was the first president of l'Alliance Nationale in 1892. Laporte's predecessor as president of the Provinciale, G.N. Ducharme, was the leading force behind the establishment of La Sauvegarde in 1901, and he was joined on its board of directors by Laporte and by Béïque and J.M. Wilson from the Hochelaga.

Upon the twenty-fifth anniversary of La Sauvegarde, Ducharme wrote that 'une nation doit être maîtresse des institutions qui reçoivent ses épargnes'; and through his activities and those of other members of the increasingly visible francophone bourgeoisie these savings were brought more and more under the control of French-run institutions during the first two decades of the century.[56] But while the French banks had ever-larger sums of money at their disposal, it was not always easy for them to find safe and profitable ways to invest their monies. In the consolidation of power over the Canadian economy into a very few hands, the largest corporations solidified their ties to the major English banks, leaving the smaller banks to deal with weaker and more vulnerable clients. The Provinciale avoided the pitfalls of making large loans to commercial and industrial firms by investing to a great degree in stocks and bonds, but even here the bank's connections to the English business community were required to get insiders' information. As for the Hochelaga and the

Nationale, the former managed to forge ties with the various Whitehead firms in the St-Maurice valley, but there were sizable loans to the Chicoutimi Pulp Company that were a cause for concern. Even more worrisome were the Nationale's ties to Paquet's factory at Montmagny. The problems created by the investments of these last two banks would ultimately lead to their merger by 1924.

6

The Establishment of the Banque Canadienne Nationale: 1921–1925

I

From its inception the structure of the Canadian banking system encouraged concentration.[1] The unrestrained establishment of branches meant that the larger institutions could easily undermine the viability of smaller ones, often forcing them either to go out of business or to accept absorption by another bank. The government rarely interceded to stop the conclusion of a merger, and in the years following World War I the concentration of power within the industry entered a new phase. While the number of banks in operation had gradually decreased from a record high of fifty-one at the start of 1875 to twenty-one in 1918, most of the institutions that passed from the scene were minor ones either located in lesser urban centres or in possession of relatively insignificant assets. From 1918 to the end of 1925 the figure was further cut to eleven, but the banks that disappeared during these years were generally institutions with long histories, numerous branches, and substantial assets. The banks which no longer existed by 1925 had been in control of 30% of total Canadian bank assets and 40% of all branches in the country at the start of 1918.

All but one of these banks passed from the scene as a result of mergers, the exception being the Home Bank, which collapsed in 1923. Six of the banks that were absorbed by a merger were acquired by the three giants of Canadian banking, the Bank of

Montreal, the Canadian Bank of Commerce, and the Royal Bank, as they vied for primacy. Long the leading force in the industry in terms of its total assets, the Bank of Montreal was temporarily overtaken by the Royal Bank during parts of 1920 and 1921. But through its acquisition of three of Montreal's oldest and largest banks, the Bank of British North America, the Merchants' Bank, and the Molson's Bank, the Bank of Montreal was securely in the lead once again by 1925.

These mergers involving hundreds of millions of dollars must have seemed part of another world to the francophone bankers, who were involved in a relatively insignificant competition among themselves and with the caisses populaires as the 1920s began. Up to this time mergers had not been responsible for reducing the number of French banks. There had been proposals to merge two or more of these banks, but none of them ever amounted to more than rhetoric. In the midst of the depression of the 1870s the Banque Jacques-Cartier entered into merger talks with both the Banque Nationale and the Banque d'Hochelaga.[2] When the Hochelaga-Jacques-Cartier proposal resurfaced in 1883 *Le Moniteur du Commerce* went even further, calling for a merger of all French banks. 'Nos banques n'apportent aucun aide à notre développement commerciale. Elles ne sont que de simples escompteurs n'ayant et ne pouvant avoir aucun rôle dans notre mouvement industriel. La fusion assurerait au profit des Canadiens [français] le développement de nos ressources et de nos industries ... L'union fait la force.'[3] In 1905 the idea of creating the single French bank was still in circulation, but the same business journal was far less enthusiastic than it had been in the 1880s, referring to the notion as a 'douce utopie' that would only lead to the destruction of the French banks.[4]

By the early 1920s, however, the idea was beginning to be taken much more seriously. Some businessmen felt that only a single, large French bank could possibly compete with the gigantic English institutions that were being produced by the merger movement. As a former manager of a Quebec branch of the Royal Bank noted, 'Pour moi la fusion de nos banques canadiennes-françaises est nécessaire au développement économique de notre

groupe. Actuellement presque toutes nos grandes maisons canadiennes-françaises sont forcées de faire affaires avec les banques
anglaises ... Aucun de ces banques – et cela de l'avis d'un direc-
teur d'une banque canadienne-française – ne pourrait à un moment donné avancer un montant considérable à une seule institution sans nuire au crédit de ses autres clients.'[5] To others such a
merger was of interest for nationalist reasons. In the aftermath of
World War I Abbé Groulx's economic nationalism had a certain
following, and one element in his message was the need for
francophones to control their own savings, an eventuality that
could be facilitated by the existence of a single strong bank.[6]

These hopes for the realization of the great merger were fuelled
by the financial crises faced by the Banque Nationale between
1921 and 1924. By late 1923 the bank's problems had become so
serious that its collapse was believed imminent. To avoid such a
disaster the provincial government entered into negotiations
with the leaders of all three French banks so as to create the single
institution that others had long desired. There had always been a
certain idealism in the various proposals for the creation of a
single powerful French bank, but there was nothing idealistic
about the negotiations that took place at the end of 1923. The
Taschereau government and its friends on the board of directors
of the Banque Nationale sought means to employ public funds to
defend their private interests, while the leaders of the Hochelaga
and the Provinciale trotted out nationalistic rhetoric to cloak their
more pragmatic concerns. Ultimately, the latter bank dropped
out of the negotiations, leaving the Hochelaga to acquire the
Nationale in 1924. The enlarged bank became the Banque Canadienne Nationale in 1925, and for the next fifty-four years it
would, along with the Provinciale, constitute the French presence in the Canadian banking industry.

II

1921 was not a good year for the banks of Canada. At the start of
the year deposits totalled nearly $1.9 billion, somewhat down
from the figure in the last months of 1920. However, this total

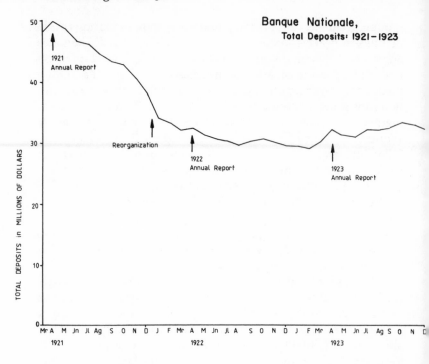

Banque Nationale,
Total Deposits: 1921–1923

would not be matched again until late in 1925. Prices collapsed under the influence of the post-war deflation, with the result that farmers, to name only one group that still had high fixed costs, were in no position to keep savings in the bank as they received less for their produce. Nowhere was this decline more evident than in the operations of the Banque Nationale, whose total deposits fell by nearly $16 million between May 1921 and February 1922. Napoléon Lavoie claimed that his bank's loss of nearly one-third of its deposits was caused 'par les besoins de la classe agricole, qui par suite de mauvaises récoltes et la baisse des prix des produits de la ferme était obligée de recouvrer ses épargnes pour vivre.'[7]

But this general problem, which touched all Canadian banks,

could not have been the sole cause for the specific crisis faced by the Nationale. Not surprisingly, the Machine Agricole account also played a role as depositors became increasingly alarmed by rumours that the Montmagny firm was about to collapse and would take the bank along with it. No one felt the impact of the Machine Agricole loans more acutely than the manager of the Nationale's Montmagny branch, who wrote in January 1922, 'Il s'est clos depuis quelques semaines 20 à 25 comptes qui ont été transportés à la Banque Royale, dû aux rumeurs malveillantes qui courrent dans le public.'[8] This account also made it next to impossible for the bank to repay its depositors. In the course of 1921 the outgoing Conservative minister of finance, Henry Drayton, provided $8.25 million in aid to the bank so that depositors might be repaid, but despite this assistance the new Liberal government still found Lavoie on its doorstep when it took power late in the year.[9] The general manager immediately entered into a lengthy correspondence with the new justice minister and former premier of Quebec, Lomer Gouin, who served as the bank's link to Ottawa over the next two years. Lavoie pointed out to Gouin that the CBA was already carrying out an investigation of the bank's affairs, but in the meantime 'ce qu'il nous faut, c'est que le gouvernement nous fasse les prêts que nous aurions besoins.'[10]

Lavoie's initial request for $1.5 million was accompanied by a justification for the bank's involvement with Machine Agricole. He admitted that the loan to this one firm tied up 'un montant énorme. Je n'entreprendrai pas d'excuser la transaction; une fois pris dans l'engrenage, l'on a eu peur de s'arrêter.' The general manager believed, however, that the money had paid for a first-rate factory and that 'si ce "plant" était anglais, on y aurait confiance, j'en suis certain.'[11] This nationalistic rhetoric was to recur upon numerous occasions and in different contexts over the next two years, but while it may have had some effect upon Gouin it clearly did not move the finance minister, W.S. Fielding, who provided only $1 million in aid. Lavoie returned to Gouin, noting that further funding was needed to avoid the failure of 'l'institution la plus canadienne-française,' and in spite of Fielding's continued coolness a further $1 million was provided to the bank.[12]

Fielding only granted this aid as a stop-gap measure to keep the bank afloat while he awaited the CBA's audit of the Nationale's books. This private report was completed in January 1922 and it provided a picture of a bank whose assets were grossly over-valued and incapable of yielding sufficient funds to repay depositors.[13] For instance, the bank listed its overdue debts as tying up only $30,000 of its funds, but the CBA's investigator set this figure at over $2.3 million. $900,000 of this amount was being falsely carried in its monthly reports to the government as 'cur-rent loans,' while the rest was hidden in its reserve fund. As for call and short loans, which the bank valued at over $7 million, many of these accounts were guaranteed by stocks and bonds of little, if any, value. Leading the way was the Machine Agricole account, whose call loans totalled $2.7 million in the bank's books, but the investigator noted that this amount 'could not be paid if payment was demanded. It should not logically be carried under this heading.'[14] Among its current loans the bank stood to lose $675,000 on its loan of $1.25 million to the Transportation and Shipping Company and a further $1.6 million on its nearly $4 million in advances to Machine Agricole. The Nationale had so much to lose in these two cases that it was accused of being 'a partner and not a banker to its clients, having in some cases much larger amounts at stake than its clients.'[15]

The CBA estimated that at the very least the bank would have to appropriate its reserve fund of $2.4 million and half of its capital of $2 million so as to purge these debts from its books. The situation was so desperate that only two options really existed.[16] Either the Nationale had to be absorbed by another bank, or it had to be completely reorganized with new capital and a strong directorate. The only party that seemed interested in the first option was the Banque d'Hochelaga, which proposed a merger of the three French banks 'on the basis of the value of their respec-tive assets.'[17] The Hochelaga stood to hold the controlling in-terest in such a merger with its assets of $72 million as opposed to $40 million for the Provinciale and probably no more than $50 million for the Nationale following the readjustment of its assets. Accordingly, the Hochelaga's general manager, Beaudry Leman, was taking no risk when he said that 'the name of the new institution, its directorate and management ... should be made the subject of a friendly discussion between the three institutions.'[18] The Hochelaga had long shown itself to be the most willing of the three banks to look for new ways to expand its operations, and its proposal can be understood in this context.

The Provinciale quickly rejected its participation in any such merger, partly because it stood to disappear under the weight of the Hochelaga and partly because it had established a reputation for handling its depositors' funds in a conservative fashion that stood to be compromised by merging with the other more adventurous French banks. So as not to appear hostile to francophone interests that seemed in danger due to the imminent collapse of the Nationale, the Provinciale couched its response in nationalistic terms. Its general manager, Tancrède Bienvenu, wrote to the president of the CBA, 'From what we know of the sentiments of our countrymen we are concerned that there would be an outburst of indignation when they find it is proposed to leave them in the hands of a single bank for all their business needs.'[19]

With the rejection of the merger plan, the CBA sought new blood to carry on the Nationale's affairs. At the end of January 1922 four new directors were named, all of whom had close ties with the Quebec premier Louis-Alexandre Taschereau, thus marking the beginning of a strong relationship between the bank and the provincial government. The most important of these new directors, Georges-Elie Amyot, was immediately chosen as the new president of the bank. Amyot was a close friend of both Taschereau and Gouin, a Liberal appointee to Quebec's Legislative Council, and the president of Dominion Corset. The bank's new vice-president, J.H. Fortier, owned two Liberal newspapers and had numerous business connections including the vice-presidency of P.T. Légaré Limitée, a wholesaling firm dealing, among other goods, in agricultural machinery. The *Financial Post* hoped that Fortier's business background would help solve the Machine Agricole problem.[20] Also appointed to the board were

Sir Georges Garneau, one-time mayor of Quebec City and formerly a Liberal nominee to the Quebec Civil Service Commission, and C.E. Taschereau, the brother of the premier. In March, Lavoie, who had already relinquished his position as general manager to Taschereau's nephew Henri des Rivières, resigned from the board, and his place was taken by Jacob Nicol. While the bank noted that Nicol was to be the Eastern Townships' representative on the board, his position as provincial treasurer was surely more relevant.[21] The bank's annual meeting in June 1922 elected ten directors, only three of whom were survivors from the board chosen a year earlier.

The CBA's investigator had noted that the Nationale's bad debts had to be purged from its books with the appropriation of all of its reserve fund and at least half of its capital, but Amyot and his friends showed no interest in reducing their investment to this extent. Shortly after entering office, they reduced the reserve fund by $2 million (leaving $400,000 intact), and moved to increase the bank's capital by $1 million (leaving all of the capital intact). The CBA had said that the reductions were essential so that confidence in the bank might be restored, but the difficulties that were faced in marketing the 10,000 new shares indicated that that confidence still did not exist. The shares were put up for sale late in March 1922, and at the annual meeting in June the directors reported that 'le montant de la nouvelle émission est couvert.'[22] In fact, as late as August only 4,201 shares had been subscribed. The remainder was sold to a group of twenty-seven men with the new directors leading the way. Even such a good friend of the bank as Lomer Gouin was reluctant to invest. In March, Amyot asked him to take on $25,000 of the new stock to 'sauver une institution canadienne-française,' but Gouin was clearly not moved by such rhetoric when it came to his own money. On 5 April, Amyot lowered his request to $10,000, and one week later Gouin reluctantly purchased $5,000 worth of new shares.[23]

Confidence in the bank was no more evident in the bank's loss of a further $4 million in deposits during the first seven months of the Amyot regime. Nor was it evident in Fielding's dealings with the new leaders, who were soon at his door seeking further loans.

The finance minister granted only $1 million of a $2.5 million loan request in late January 1922, and was clearly ill at ease in advancing even this amount. He wrote to the president of the CBA, 'You have repeatedly pointed out that the failure of the Banque Nationale would be a disaster of a widespread character, affecting the banking system generally ... It seems to me that in view of the interest of all banks in this matter it is not too much to ask the large banks to do something themselves, rather than have the Banque Nationale turn always to the Government for aid.'[24] Fielding was even less charitable when Amyot requested a $2-million deposit to inflate the bank's status at the end of its 1921–2 fiscal year. Amyot promised to return the funds in June, but Fielding would have no part of it. Gouin tried to intercede and received for his efforts 'la plus belle rebuffade de [sa] vie.'[25]

In spite of these setbacks, Amyot tried to paint a positive picture at the bank's annual meeting in June 1923. 'Nous pouvons tous ensemble envisager l'avenir avec confiance. Les gages de ce progrès désiré sont visibles de nos yeux.'[26] One can only assume that Amyot was looking through rose-coloured glasses. Although the bank operated with nearly $1 million more capital in 1922–3 than it had had during 1921–2, its net profits declined and as a percentage of paid capital stood well below the norm for banks of its size. By the end of April 1923 the bank's deposits had almost returned to their level at the time of the 1922 annual meeting, but this was only achieved through an increase of $2 million in deposits during the month of April. Some observers saw in this increase the hand of the Taschereau government trying to improve the bank's image before the closing of its books for the year on 30 April. This was the sort of ploy with which Fielding had refused to be involved in 1922, but the provincial government's participation was evident in several ways. First, the province's own balance with the bank increased from $633,000 at the end of March to $2.13 million at the end of April, only to return to $1.2 million in May. In addition, among the bank's deposits from the public substantial sums were reported to have been left by municipalities and school boards during April on the instructions of the Taschereau government.[27] Following the close of the fiscal year these deposits fell by nearly $1 million in the course of May.

The bank's difficulties in earning solid profits and in retaining its depositors' funds were no doubt linked to the inability of the Amyot team to resolve the Machine Agricole problem. At roughly the same time that the new leaders were taking charge of the Banque Nationale, Charles Paquet was on his way out as president of the Montmagny firm. In January 1922 Paquet wrote a desperate letter to Gouin asking him to put in a good word with Amyot and seeking government contracts. As Paquet put it, the alternative would be 'une catastrophe rentissante et une humiliation pour notre race.'[28] Such emotional pleas did not bring further aid from either Gouin or the bank, and in late February Paquet closed down his factory, turning it over to the trust company which held the mortgage on the plant in the name of the bearers of $4 million of Machine Agricole bonds. Paquet could no longer pay the interest on the bonds, the majority of which were held by the bank, and by the terms of the bond issue he relinquished control of the property.

The bank suffered from these events in various ways. There was the continued impression among the public that the collapse of Machine Agricole would lead to the fall of its major creditor, the Banque Nationale. At the same time people in the Montmagny area, particularly those who had purchased $700,000 of Machine Agricole bonds through branches of the bank, were angered by the fact that the bank would not provide further aid to keep the factory open. Accordingly, in the two weeks following the plant's closing, the bank's Montmagny manager noted the loss of $12,000 in deposits because of the 'impression plutôt hostile à la banque.'[29] The factory reopened in April 1922, essentially under the direction of the bank, with a view to finishing orders already begun, but it was clear that unless the bondholders were willing to put up more money or a buyer could be found it would never return to full production. This uncertainty became a further source of problems for the bank. When a rumour was spread in October 1922 that the plant was to be permanently closed, there was a run by depositors upon the

bank's branch at Montmagny. The manager there, Prudent Vallée, wrote at the start of the run, 'Bien des gens croient que la
faillite de la Machine Agricole entrainerait à sa suite, celle de la
Banque Nationale. Ils croient par conséquent leur argent en
danger.'[30] During the month of November alone the branch lost
nearly 2,000 accounts with deposits of over $400,000.[31] In addi-
tion, the bank lost its manager, Vallée, who suffered a nervous
breakdown during the run and retired from the bank.[32]

In spite of its problems at Montmagny the bank's affairs did not
appreciably deteriorate in the months following Amyot's decep-
tively positive report in the spring of 1923. What did change,
however, was the attitude of the federal government towards the
bank. As has already been seen, Fielding was not a great sup-
porter of the Nationale. Nevertheless, from early 1922 up to the
summer of 1923 he willingly ignored the fact that the bank's
assets were grossly overvalued. He had read the CBA's report, but
so as to avoid a loss of the shareholders' investment he did not
force the bank to readjust its assets, reduce its capital, or
appropriate its reserve. All of this changed, however, with the
collapse of the Home Bank in August 1923. The depositors of this
bank stood to lose $20 million, and calls emerged for stricter
government supervision of the banks. The Liberal government
could hardly afford another bank failure, and in November Fielding ordered a further investigation into the Nationale's affairs.[33]
The results were no surprise to the minister when it was found
that the Machine Agricole bonds were still being carried at par
and that various loans were, to use Amyot's expression, 'considerably exaggerated.'[34]

In the changed atmosphere following the Home Bank collapse
Fielding was no longer going to tolerate these misrepresentations, but Amyot knew that to reduce the assets would lead to a
further run on the bank that could not be supported. Accordingly, it was a panicky Amyot who rushed to New York in early
December 1923 to apprise Gouin, who was returning from
Europe, of the latest crisis. Gouin, suffering from poor health and
soon to resign from the cabinet, said that he could not act before
the reconvening of Parliament, which was three months away.

Unable to wait, Amyot then turned to Taschereau, who had been the bank's best friend since the reorganization. Apparently without any reluctance Taschereau committed himself to preventing the failure of the bank. He was prepared to put the provincial treasury at the disposal of the other two banks to facilitate their acquisition of the Nationale. From that moment the history of the Banque Nationale was, to all intents and purposes, at an end. The only questions that remained pertained to the cost to be incurred by the government and to the nature of the involvement of the Hochelaga and the Provinciale.

III

Negotiations between Taschereau and the leaders of the three banks took place in complete secrecy during the last two weeks of 1923. All that is known of these talks is that the Provinciale refused to be a party to any merger. Accordingly, the deal that was struck was essentially one between the provincial government and the Banque d'Hochelaga. The full details of the arrangement for the Hochelaga's takeover of the Nationale were first made public with the tabling of Bill 3 in the provincial legislature in mid-January.[35] The government committed itself to conveying to the Hochelaga $15 million in provincial bonds. These bonds, paying 5% interest and maturing in forty years, could be sold at any time so as to constitute a liquid asset for the Hochelaga, which was absorbing the heavy responsibilities of the Nationale. In return, the bank was to give back the interest on the bonds to the government and to make an annual payment of nearly $125,000 which, capitalized at the rate of 5% per year, would cover the principal of the bonds by the time of their maturity. The Hochelaga was only obliged to make these payments out of its profits, and only after a 10% dividend had been paid to its shareholders. Bill 3 further specified that the Hochelaga was to provide one share of its own stock for two Banque Nationale shares and to redeem at face value the $680,000 of Machine Agricole bonds that the Nationale had sold through its branches.

There were few who doubted that some action was needed to

protect the depositors of the Banque Nationale. While governments were able to stand by and watch the collapse of the Banque du Peuple, they could hardly do the same in the case of the Nationale, whose deposits in 1923 were roughly ten times those of the Banque du Peuple in 1895. The federal government, which provided $3 million in aid to depositors of the Home Bank in 1925, was apparently not interested in participating in this case, thus leaving the field to the Quebec government.[36] This does not explain, however, why the province had to invest $15 million in order to achieve this limited end upon terms that provided the Hochelaga with the possibility of avoiding repayment. The Banque d'Hochelaga (after 1925 the Banque Canadienne Nationale) subsequently paid back its debt to the government, but this could not have been taken for granted in early 1924 when even the Hochelaga's own status was, as we shall see, shaky. Given the possibility that the $15 million might never be repaid, one less expensive alternative that presumably presented itself to the government was to allow the Nationale to go under, and then to provide compensation to depositors. The bank's assets at the start of 1924 had a market value of $36 million, while the liabilities (not including its capital and reserve) stood at $48 million. One-quarter of this shortfall of $12 million could have been covered by invoking the double liability clause, while a further $400,000 could have come from the reserve. In this fashion all of the depositors could have been paid in full at a cost to the province of less than $6 million.

It is unlikely, however, that the Taschereau government ever considered this alternative because of all of the parties that would have been hurt in the process. To begin with, there were the shareholders, who would have not only lost their investment but would have also been forced to pay compensation to the bank's creditors. Taschereau claimed that he could not allow this to happen to the 2,300 shareholders that included in their number widows, orphans, and nuns.[37] In fact, only 10% of the bank's shares in 1921 were held by such people; the vast majority rested in the hands of professionals or businessmen. At the start of 1924 the widows could have received the face value of $100 for their stock at a cost of only $300,000 to the state. Instead, a deal was worked out with the Hochelaga whereby each investor in the Nationale received Hochelaga stock with a market value of $75 for shares that had not even traded on the Montreal Stock Exchange in the last months of 1923. Moreover, the Nationale shareholders, who had benefited from high dividends while bad debts were allowed to sit on the bank's books, were now guaranteed a dividend of 10% before any payment on the $15 million had to be made.

Taschereau also acted to reimburse the Machine Agricole bondholders among whose number he found 900 people living on meagre incomes.[38] Why this clause was even inserted in Bill 3 was incomprehensible to some observers. While the bonds had been sold through offices of the Nationale, they had been issued by an industrial concern that had long shown itself incapable of managing its own affairs. Accordingly, Henri Bourassa saw their redemption at par as 'une prime à la maladministration.'[39] If the government felt sorry for these bondholders they could have been compensated without the participation of the Hochelaga at a cost of only $680,000. In any event, it would appear that all of the people about whom Taschereau claimed to be so concerned did not receive the benefit of this aid. Only hours after the deal was announced *Le Soleil* noted that 'certaines personnes [parcouraient] les campagnes cherchant à acquérir les obligations de la Machine Agricole de Montmagny, à des prix beaucoup audessous de leur valeur actuelle.'[40] Many urged Taschereau to amend Bill 3 so as to prevent this speculation that took the benefit of the act from those for whom it was intended, but the premier was curiously uninterested.

All of the depositors, the indigent shareholders, and the Machine Agricole bondholders could have been paid off at a cost of less than $10 million, and even if all of the Nationale's shareholders were compensated the figure would still have come to only $12.28 million. Instead, the government chose to invest $15 million to have the Banque d'Hochelaga incur these expenses with no certainty that the investment would be repaid. Taschereau further justified his actions by noting the need to protect the clients of the Nationale whose firms might have fallen had the bank been left to collapse. 'La Banque Nationale especially finances small French Canadian industries and commercial houses who in turn are the clients of the big houses in Quebec and Montreal ... [which] have absolute need of this clientele to exist and get through the world crisis which has lasted several years and which threatens to continue.'[41] The premier did not mention, however, that the viable clients of the Nationale would have ultimately found accommodation with other banks as had been the case following the other French bank failures. As for the Nationale's weak clients, there is no evidence that the Hochelaga did anything to help them survive.[42] The failure of the Nationale would have resulted in an end of credit to these customers and a demand for repayment by the bank's liquidators, two actions that could have led to numerous bankruptcies. With $15 million at its disposal to purge bad debts from its books, the Hochelaga had lttle incentive to continue these accounts, lest their collected debt exceed $15 million.

In the final analysis, the government issued $15 million in bonds to allow the Hochelaga to secure the depositors' money and the investments of others, and to write off the debts of the Nationale which would have been equally worthless if no action had been taken. This $15-million figure was set by the Hochelaga so that after the takeover of the Nationale its liquid assets might equal 50% of its liabilities to the public. The bank claimed that this figure was generally respected by all responsible bankers, and Taschereau claimed to have received independent confirmation of this fact by submitting the balance sheets of the two banks to 'disinterested bankers' whose names he did not provide.[43] According to the Hochelaga's own rather curious definition of liquid assets, which included corporate securities which were not always easily negotiable, its liquid assets equalled 51% of its liabilities to the public at the start of December 1923.[44] The Nationale's figure was 41% if the Machine Agricole bonds were included, and 31% if they were seen as worthless, but the government accepted the Hochelaga's claim that a further $6.6 million of miscellaneous municipal and foreign securities were also of no

TABLE 6.1
Liquid assets of Banque d'Hochelaga and Banque Nationale, 30 November 1923

	A: Liquid assets (millions of $)	B: Liabilities to public (millions of $)	A as % of B
Hochelaga's figures			
Hochelaga	32	63.2	51
Nationale	8	47.8	17
After merger with			
$15 million in bonds	55	111.0	50
Based on likely market value of securities			
Hochelaga	32	63.2	51
Nationale	14.7	47.8	30
After merger with			
$15 million in bonds	61.7	111.0	56

Source: *Le Devoir*, 21 January 1924

value so as to reduce the Nationale's ratio to only 17%.[45] There is no evidence that these last-mentioned securities were without value, but it was only with such an assumption that the government could justify the $15-million figure. Assuming that these securities were worth their reported value, the Hochelaga stood to raise its own percentage to 56%, well above the figure of 47% for the industry as a whole.

Throughout this affair Taschereau steadfastly refused to shed light on his motivations for providing the precise form of aid specified in Bill 3. Henri Bourassa forcefully pushed for the establishment of a parliamentary committee to bring out the details. The premier rejected the proposal, noting that time was of the essence if the failure of the Nationale was to be avoided. Bourassa could not understand, however, why the bill needed to be pushed through in mid-January when the shareholders of the two banks were not going to meet to approve the government's proposal until 21 February. Bill 3 was introduced on 17 January and had already received third reading by 24 January. *Le Devoir*'s director noted, 'Ce railroading ... n'est pas de nature à impressionner favorablement les observateurs désintéressés.'[46]

Given the questions that could be asked about the costs that might eventually be incurred by the state, it is hardly surprising that this absence of information provoked considerable cynicism in certain quarters. Singled out for attention was the generous settlement with the shareholders of the Nationale, among whose number were Taschereau's friends on the board of directors who had granted themselves considerable loans in the last months of the bank's existence.[47] Bourassa complained 'que [le gouvernement] subordonne les droits de la province aux profits des actionnaires de la Banque Nationale, c'est injustifiable.'[48] The leader of the opposition in the Legislative Assembly, Arthur Sauvé, went even further. 'Les petits épargnants, les déposants, l'avantage de fonder une banque française puissante, cela, c'est le paravent, c'est le prétexte, c'est le poudre pour les yeux. Le motif, le vrai, c'est le désir du gouvernement d'épargner à ses amis une catastrophe … Et c'est là le côté scandaleux de l'affaire.'[49]

Taschereau responded to these critics by claiming to be above such petty motives. In regard to the charges that he had acted to aid his friends and relatives, he remarked, 'I [would] not sully my name, nor tarnish my reputation for so little.'[50] He also pointed out that the gain of a few thousand dollars was insignificant to men as wealthy as Amyot.[51] By answering his critics in such a manner, however, Taschereau avoided the hard questions that were being asked. None of the critics doubted that something had to be done by the province, even though it was rare for governments, either federal or provincial, to take direct action in such cases. The critics accepted the fact that the depositors needed to be protected, but they wondered whether the shareholders also warranted support at a potentially considerable cost to the provincial treasury. The premier decided that the shareholders deserved a better fate than being forced to meet their double liability to the creditors, but given the bank's management in its last years one wonders why. The government's ties to the board of the Banque Nationale did not by themselves move it to act, but once action was to be taken these ties increased the potential costs involved. Taschereau was determined that another bank should acquire the Nationale so as to protect the shareholders' investment, and when the Provinciale dropped out of the picture he was forced to accept the price, no matter how inflated, set by the Hochelaga.

IV

The Quebec government, facing the imminent demise of the Banque Nationale, sought to work out a deal with the two French banks, but while the Hochelaga willingly participated the Provinciale wanted no part of the affair. Both banks, however, tried to justify their decisions by noting the selflessness of their actions. At the meeting of shareholders called to approve the Hochelaga's participation, Beaudry Leman commented, 'Nous n'avons jamais ambitionné d'édifier notre prospérité sur les misères ou les difficultés des autres. Nous avons préféré nous inspirer de l'exemple du Samaritain qui aide son prochain avec simplicité.'[52] As for the Provinciale, it believed, as it had in 1922, that one French bank was not in the best interests of the French Canadian people. Hormisdas Laporte argued, 'Une seule banque française serait insuffisante et au détriment de l'expansion industrielle et commerciale de notre Race.'[53]

Both banks tried to exploit the public relations aspects of their decisions, but their actions were shaped by more pragmatic concerns than issues of nationalism. Some observers suggested that the Hochelaga worked out a deal with the government because of the strong Liberal leanings of its directors. By contrast, several of the Provinciale's leaders, including Laporte, were Conservatives, and there were even rumours that Bienvenu had blocked participation because Taschereau had denied him a seat on the Legislative Council.[54]

Realistically, however, neither bank would have acted in a manner harmful to its business interests simply for political reasons. Both responded to the prospect of taking over the Nationale in a way that was consistent with the nature of their operations. For the Provinciale in 1923, as had been the case in 1922, there could be no question of involving itself in the affairs of a bank that had been as loose with its depositors' funds as the Nationale. For two decades since the passing from the scene of the Banque Jacques-Cartier, the Provinciale had invested heavily in call loans and in various securities so as to protect the savings of its clients. This practice continued to provide the bank with solid profits into the 1920s, and there was no way that the bank's leaders were going to abandon a successful system, even in the face of government aid.

The Hochelaga, by contrast, had no reason to object to a merger with the Nationale based on the structure of its business. While the Hochelaga may have dealt with a higher class of customers than did the Quebec City bank, both dabbled infrequently in call loans and stocks and bonds, and both had relatively low liquidity ratios when compared to that of the Provinciale. Accordingly, the Hochelaga would have been prepared to absorb the Nationale in 1922 had the Provinciale been interested in joining in, and when government assistance was made available in 1923 it did not hesitate to accept it.

Under the leadership of men such as F.L. Béïque, the Banque d'Hochelaga had shown itself willing to try to expand in a variety of ways, and the absorption of the Nationale was simply another example of this orientation. Béïque had helped gain several large industrial accounts for the bank and had led its drive to establish itself in English markets in the prairies. Accordingly, it is not entirely surprising that following the absorption of the Nationale the Hochelaga sought to change its name to the Banque Canadienne Nationale (BCN), a title which would reflect its 'sphère d'action,' which was all of Canada and not merely Quebec.[55] This decision disappointed certain nationalists such as Abbé Groulx who hoped that the new name would be the Banque Nationale du Québec, and they were to be disappointed again when Leman and his colleagues sought federal approval to use the English translation of the name so as to gain English clients more easily. Anatole Vanier, a colleague of Groulx, complained that 'une fraction importante de vos déposants voient dans la traduction d'un nom français un manque de dignité et de solidarité de la part d'une institution française.'[56] These complaints aside, the Hochelaga became the Banque Canadienne Nationale/Bank Canadian National in February 1925.

The Hochelaga's eagerness to expand also played a role, however, in the size of the investment that the province had to make for the bank's takeover of the Nationale. By lending out the bulk of their depositors' funds to a small number of clients, both banks ran the risk that the failure of their larger accounts could leave them unable to repay depositors. This came to pass because of the Nationale's dealings with Machine Agricole, and a potentially similar situation faced the Hochelaga late in 1923 because of its dealings with the Saguenay Pulp and Power Company, of which Béïque was the president. By the close of 1923 the bank held roughly $1.75 million in Saguenay Pulp and Power bonds, $750,000 of which it held outright and another $1 million which it held as security for various loans.[57] In addition, the bank made advances that reached $700,000 in the course of 1923 to Saguenay Pulp and Power's major subsidiary, the Chicoutimi Pulp Company.[58] These last advances were made on the security of orders from the English firm of Becker and Company, which marketed the firm's entire output. Becker also handled the production of the Bay Sulphite Company, 45% of whose stock was owned by Chicoutimi Pulp.

When Becker failed in early November 1923 there were serious consequences both for the firms associated with Saguenay Pulp and Power and for the banks that supported them. Both Chicoutimi Pulp and Bay Sulphite were forced into liquidation, leaving their creditors with worthless paper in their vaults. The Molson's Bank had to write off its investments in Saguenay Pulp and Power first by appropriating its reserve fund of $2 million and subsequently by accepting the merger offer of the Bank of Montreal.[59] The Hochelaga, which was paying for the day to day operations of Chicoutimi Pulp at the close of 1923, was more fortunate, however, because it had the provincial government to help it. The bank sought to improve its liquidity position as much as possible at the time of the merger not only to absorb the dubious investments of the Nationale but also to purge its own bad debts from its books. La Ligue de protection des épargnes de la province de Québec, a group for the promotion of the caisse populaire movement, had no reason to be kind to the banks. Nevetheless, its observations regarding the merger tended to be right on the mark. It noted that 'les débentures [de la Saguenay Pulp and Power] avec ceux de Bay Sulphite sont enfouies dans les voûtes de la Banque d'Hochelaga comme celles de la Machine Agricole le sont dans celles de la Banque Nationale.'[60] Beaudry Leman claimed that the $15 million was 'pour protéger les déposants et les créanciers de la Banque Nationale. La Banque d'Hochelaga n'avait et n'a besoin d'aucun secours.'[61] By contrast, the Ligue de protection referred to the merger as 'la liquidation plus voilée de l'Hochelaga,' and given the way in which the bank juggled figures so as to justify $15 million in support this seems perfectly plausible.[62]

v

There were considerable differences in the way in which the last two French banks invested their funds. Nevertheless, both received their monies from the same pool of savings, and with the passing from the scene of the Nationale the Hochelaga and the Provinciale settled in to compete for the francophone Quebec market. Following the merger, the Hochelaga had 305 branches under its control, a number that it reduced to 263 within a year. In the process, numerous towns that were served by two banks became one-bank communities, and the Provinciale quickly geared up to replace the closed offices of the Nationale. Only two weeks after the announcement of the merger and well before the passage of Bill 3, Bienvenu reported to his directors that 'the merger ... will create many opportunities for the opening of new branches where both of these institutions were formerly in competition,' and authorization was given for the opening of a dozen new branches.[63] Bienvenu even wrote to Napoléon Lavoie, the former general manager of the Nationale, to gain his knowledge about prospects in these towns.[64] Not surprisingly, these actions infuriated the leaders of the Hochelaga, whose president, J.A. Vaillancourt, wrote to Laporte: 'Serait-il juste ou même simplement honnête que nous soyons maintenant privés d'une partie des revenus qui seraient nécessaires à l'exécution du program que nous nous sommes tracés, auquel vous avez été invités par le gouvernement à participer, dans lequel vous avez refusé de prendre votre part, et dont vous voudriez maintenant ... obtenir tous les avantages possibles.'[65]

Having failed in their attempts to penetrate the English market, the two French banks were prepared to wage an all-out war for the savings of francophone Quebecers. At the start of 1925, at the time that the Hochelaga was about to become the BCN, the total deposits of the two banks were $121 million, only 7% of the total for the industry. In the short term each could only look to the savings of the other as a means to expand, but cooler heads soon prevailed as the leaders of the two institutions added up the cost of establishing branches in a war to the death. Talks were begun to reduce the competition between the two banks where the market required fewer branches, and between July 1925 and May 1926 nearly sixty offices were closed by mutual agreement.[66]

As the leaders of the last two French banks were painfully aware, in the context of the Canadian banking industry they were still relatively insignificant players with only 6% of total Canadian bank assets at the start of 1925. In the context of the Quebec economy, however, these banks had become institutions of major importance because of their control over a substantial portion of the savings of the francophone population. The caisses populaires were still relatively insignificant, while the English banks still concentrated their operations in communities with important English populations. By the close of 1923 the Banque Nationale had 23,000 depositors, and no government in Quebec City could allow so many people to lose their savings. While there were many aspects of Taschereau's actions in the Banque Nationale affair that raised eyebrows, no one objected to the principle of aiding the depositors. The first French bank, the Banque du Peuple, had been seen by some as an enemy to the state, but by 1924 the French banks played such a major role in the economy of Quebec that they were in a position to command the support of the state.

7

Conclusion

The renewal of interest in the history of Canadian banking over the past decade has largely been the result of the appearance of Tom Naylor's *History of Canadian Business*.[1] Naylor drew others into this field through his assertion that the banks played the central role in the underdevelopment of certain regions and of certain sectors of the economy. He displayed an unbridled enthusiasm for the American system of unit banking and assumed that if numerous locally controlled banks had existed across Canada, industrial growth would have been more impressive and regional disparities less pronounced.[2] In Naylor's view of the economy, the banks played the role of independent variables capable of bringing about major transformations. To build up the role of the banks, he pushed aside the impact of other variables such as technology, geography, and a host of market factors.

The operations of the French banks between 1835 and 1925 provided little support for Naylor's views. To be sure, these banks occupied a relatively marginal place within the industry and were unlikely to be able to bring about major transformations in the Quebec economy. Nevertheless, there are glimpses from their operations to indicate that they were far from being hostile towards industrial projects.[3] As for the role that these banks played in moving funds from certain regions of the province to the more developed areas such as Montreal, the evidence is clear. In 1921, for instance, the Banque d'Hochelaga's main branch in

Montreal recorded a surplus of loans over deposits of nearly $8 million, while its other offices in Quebec saw deposits in the lead by over $11 million.[4] One would be wrong, however, to assume that this situation was somehow endemic to the Canadian banking industry. The caisses populaires, for instance, were designed to mobilize and reinvest savings within a single parish, but inevitably some parishes had excess savings while others required further capital to satisfy the demand for credit. Desjardins' solution was to propose the establishment of a *caisse centrale* which would, ironically, operate much like the head office of the chartered banks which he disliked so intensely.[5]

The point of this study has not been, however, to try either to prove or disprove the Naylor thesis regarding the role of the banks as agents of change. Rather, the approach has been to look at the French banks as dependent variables, whose histories reflected profound changes in the economy and society of Quebec. For instance, the history of these banks mirrored the evolution of the province from its reliance upon a relatively unproductive form of farming in 1835 to its emergence as an urban-industrial society with a sophisticated agricultural sector by the early 1900s. Along the way, some of the province's francophone population accumulated sufficient savings both to invest and deposit funds in the French banks. While all of the early French institutions required considerable amounts of English capital either to start up or to expand, this situation was changing by the late nineteenth century and in the early 1900s nearly all of the new investment in the surviving French banks came from francophones. In addition, the French banks followed the pattern for the industry as a whole by establishing numerous branches through which the savings of francophone Quebecers might be tapped. In the early 1900s these savings were sufficient to allow the savings deposits of the French banks to increase at a much faster rate than did those for the industry as a whole. Historian Bernard Vigod has claimed that 'French Canadians invariably preferred to deal with the English banks, as depositors, borrowers and investors,' but if that was their preference it was not borne out by their actions.[6]

TABLE 7.1
Francophone investors and the French banks,
1871–1921

Year	% Investment in French banks coming from francophones
1871	62
1881	65
1891	72
1901	85
1911	86
1921	89

Source: See appendix II.

TABLE 7.2
Selected occupations of the directors of the Quebec banks, 1835–1925

	Professionals and merchants			Manufacturers and financiers		
	1835–73	1874–99	1900–25	1835–73	1874–99	1900–25
English banks	58%	48	34	24	31	52
French banks	75%	64	55	13	20	29

Source: See appendix III.

The history of these banks also reflected certain changes in the francophone bourgeoisie. The earliest directors of the French banks were men who largely identified themselves as merchants, who had few interests that transcended the boundaries of Quebec, and who were involved in few other enterprises. With the changes in the Quebec economy during the late nineteenth century, this profile began to change. Brian Young has shown the rise of industrial and financial interests in his description of the decline of the political fortunes of George-Etienne Cartier in the 1870s.[7] Similarly, on the boards of the French banks men with a wide array of business interests such as G.C. Dessaulles of the Banque de St-Hyacinthe and Alphonse Desjardins of the Banque

Jacques-Cartier became more prominent. In the early twentieth century the decline of the merchants continued with the appearance of a few men who rubbed shoulders with the major players in the Canadian economy. Most notable in this last group were Rodolphe Forget of the Banque Provinciale and, of course, F.L. Béïque of the Hochelaga.

While the percentage of directors of the French banks who identified themselves primarily as merchants declined across this period, the figure remained considerably higher than it was for the English banks. Similarly, despite the increased importance of manufacturers and financiers among French bank directors, these percentages were consistently lower than those for the English institutions. These differences were indicative of the invariably marginal place of the francophone bourgeoisie within the larger Canadian economy. Forget and Béïque were exceptional participants in the consolidation of monopoly capitalism due to their wealth and connections. Their involvement indicated that it was possible for a francophone to enter the highest levels of Canadian business, but few of their compatriots could hope to have the necessary credentials.

The history of the French banks indicated that francophone enterprise was capable of considerable growth, but only within the confines of the limited French-speaking market. Accordingly, it should come as little surprise if the bulk of the leaders of these institutions had similarly limited business interests. In this regard, the directors of the French banks were not unlike the leaders of the smaller English banks of the province. For instance, among Quebec banks that operated throughout the period from 1874 to 1899, professionals and merchants comprised the majority of directors for all but three institutions. These three, the Bank of Montreal, the Molson's Bank, and the Merchants' Bank, were the largest in the province at the turn of the century. By contrast, banks such as the Eastern Townships Bank were led by men of limited means and operated within narrowly defined boundaries. In the early 1900s the Sherbrooke-based bank, not constrained by the linguistic barriers faced by the French banks, tried to extend its operations across Canada, but its directors could not hope to compete with the leaders of the Canadian economy and in 1912 the bank was absorbed by the Canadian Bank of Commerce.

In addition to the similarities in the backgrounds of the directors of Quebec's smaller banks, French and English alike, there were also parallels in the day-to-day operations of these banks. While there were considerable differences between the affairs of the larger institutions and those of the smaller ones, language played a relatively minor role in influencing most aspects of a bank's operations. This is hardly surprising given the considerable differences that often existed in the way that the various French banks operated. Accordingly, for Quebec-based banks there was essentially no relationship between the language of a bank's operations and the profitability of its affairs across the period from 1857 to 1925. On the other hand, there was a moderately strong correlation between the size of a bank, whether English or French, and its profits, with the larger banks earning the greater returns. The larger banks also tended to pay higher dividends and to build up larger reserve funds (calculated as a percentage of paid capital). Once more, there was only a relatively weak relationship between language and the operations of the bank.[8]

These parallels in the affairs of all of Quebec's smaller banks, French and English alike, were also evident in the evolution of their liabilities and assets. For the banking industry in general, the period from 1857 to 1925 saw a decline in the importance of shareholders' funds as a percentage of total liabilities and a corresponding increase in the role of savings deposits. Among Quebec banks, however, the larger institutions generally relied less upon shareholders' contributions and more upon those of depositors than did the smaller banks. There was a much less important association between a bank's language of operations and the distribution of its liabilities.

Owing to their growing dependence upon savings deposits, Canadian banks increasingly needed to place their monies in investment with a high likelihood of yielding funds on short notice. Accordingly, across this period current loans decreased in importance among total assets with their place being taken by call loans and cash items. The smaller banks of Quebec tended to tie up a larger percentage of their assets in current loans and a smaller portion in call loans than was the case for the larger banks. Since the larger banks employed their resources to establish numerous branches and to take in considerable savings deposits, it is not surprising that they were more conscious of keeping their assets in a liquid state than were the smaller banks. As for the language of the bank, it was once more of scarcely any importance.

In terms of all these aspects of bank operations, the size of the institution was more important than the language spoken in the boardroom. This is not to say, however, that there was a perfect relationship between the value of a bank's assets and the nature of its affairs. Certainly among the French banks there were numerous examples of institutions of a comparable size operating in very different fashions. The affairs of these banks were influenced not only by the scale of their operations but also by less quantifiable factors such as the history of the institutions and the connections of their leaders. For instance, the early operations of the Banque du Peuple make no sense if one ignores the historical circumstances under which it was founded; nor do the operations of the Banque Provinciale during the first quarter of the twentieth century make any sense if the history of the Banque Jacques-Cartier is forgotten. As for the influence of the leaders of these banks, one only has to compare the Banque d'Hochelaga and the Banque Nationale. The two institutions each had total assets of nearly identical values at the start of the 1920s. Nevertheless, their affairs were very different, due in large part to the fact that F.L. Béïque had ties to Canada's business elite while Rodolphe Audette was a man of merely regional business concerns.

While the value of a bank's assets could not completely determine the nature of an institution's affairs, size did tend to be considerably more important than language in all but one regard. The only major difference that emerged between the operations of the smaller English banks of Quebec and those of their French counterparts was the market which each group chose to pursue, particularly in terms of savings deposits. These English institutions started off by dealing with English clients within the province, but they all ended up by also looking for English-speaking customers beyond Quebec. There were three such banks at the turn of the century, the Eastern Townships Bank, the Quebec Bank, and the Union Bank. The first two could not afford to keep up an expensive competition with the larger banks and were absorbed through mergers, while the Union Bank left Quebec in 1912 to attend to its growing western business from its new headquarters in Winnipeg. However, even this last institution was ultimately taken over by the Royal Bank in 1925. The French banks, by contrast, secured a French clientele, both within Quebec and outside the province. Some francophone leaders worried that by the 1920s too much French money was going to the English banks, but if that had been so the French institutions would have most likely collapsed as a result of their inability to make a dent in the English market. The French banks had a solid clientele which assured their survival. However, the limitations of this market prevented them from ever being more than minor players within the Canadian banking industry.

Such market considerations have rarely occupied an important place, however, in the considerable literature that has tried to explain the marginal place of francophones within the Canadian economy. French-speaking businessmen allegedly were fearful of success, were poor judges of markets, or were too reluctant to take risks or to take on partners, to cite only a few of the more commonly employed explanations.[9] The history of the French banks provided no support for these claims which assumed that francophone entrepreneurs had an inappropriate *mentalité* that precluded their success. The French banks largely functioned as did other banks of their size. If their 'Frenchness' had any role to play in their operations, it was in permitting them to maintain a market during a period of consolidation within the Canadian economy. In this sense, the continued existence of two French banks in 1925 was due to the fact that they were French.

APPENDICES
NOTES
BIBLIOGRAPHY
INDEX

Appendices

All the information in this study pertaining to bank assets and liabilities comes from the *Canada Gazette*. Beginning in late 1856 and continuing to the present, the *Gazette* has provided monthly reports on the operations of Canada's banks based on data supplied by the banks themselves. This is an indispensable source for anyone serious about understanding the way in which the banks collected their funds and invested them. Nevertheless, there are problems involved in using these data. To begin with, from 1856 to 1867 only the banks of the province of Canada were included in the *Gazette*'s tables, but even after Confederation the Maritime banks only gradually complied with the government's request for information. According to C.A. Curtis, whose explanation of the pitfalls of this source is essential reading for anyone wishing to use it, complete coverage only began in 1890.[1] Further problems arise from the fact that the categories employed to indicate the breakdown of assets and liabilities changed considerably over time. In 1861, for instance, there were only seven different categories for the types of assets held by the banks, a figure that increased to 28 by 1921. Curtis' work is indispensable on this issue, since he provided a table to show how these categories evolved over time.

The *Canada Gazette* data raise still another problem, however, that Curtis did not even consider. It must be remembered that the banks were on their honour to submit accurate returns, and there are numerous examples in the histories of the French banks to indicate that the government's rather naïve trust was occasionally betrayed. There were even cases in which the government knew that inaccurate returns were being submitted, but did little to set the banks straight. The Banque de St-Jean, for instance, seemingly reported a paid capital that was well above the amount actually paid throughout most of its history, while the Banque Ville-Marie knowingly underestimated the real value of its notes in circulation.[2] Similarly, the Banque Nationale placed certain loans with little security in the call loans category in the early 1920s so as to give a false impression of the liquidity of its assets. The federal government knew of this situation early in 1922, but did nothing to act until the collapse of the Home Bank late in 1923.[3] The fall of this last bank, whose returns were also of dubious accuracy, brought calls for the establishment of a separate office to watch over bank operations. This study ends at roughly the same time that the position of Inspector General of Banks came into existence, so that it is impossible to say whether the bank returns were improved in the process.

It would be easy to dismiss the *Canada Gazette* data as worthless because of the misrepresentations that evidently did exist. However, the fact remains that this is the only statistical series regarding the operations of all banks that exists, and if one uses it carefully it can still offer useful insights. Throughout this study, whenever it was possible, the reported data were altered if they contradicted well-founded information unearthed elsewhere. Such double-checking was particularly important in coming to grips with the real status of the Banque Nationale as it teetered on the brink of collapse in the early 1920s. In other less infamous cases the need for double-checking was not always obvious. However, in those cases there was protection from the occasional false report in the fact that much of this information was used as part of various time series. Accordingly, a single outrageous report could be easily identified and confirmed. Relatively minor inaccuracies would take on little importance in such statistical series.

Out of the massive amount of data available from the *Canada Gazette*, a very specific set of information was collected for careful analysis. Data regarding selected aspects of the assets and liabilities of Quebec-based banks were collected from the returns for January from 1857 to 1925. This information forms the basis for all comparisons that are made in the text between the French banks and other Quebec-based institutions. In certain places in the text, one will find one of the French banks compared to other Quebec banks of the same size. The comparison was achieved by grouping the banks into six categories based upon the value of their total assets. Accordingly, the Banque de St-Jean, whose total assets were $573,352 in 1897, would have been compared to other banks with total assets of less than $1 million. The other five categories placed the banks into groups with total assets of $1 to $5 million, $5 to $10 million, $10 to $25 million, $25 to $100 million, and more than $100 million. Any such system is open to the charge of being arbitrary, but this scheme divided the banks into groups that had very different scales of operations.

In other cases, the French banks were compared as a group with the rest of the Quebec-based institutions over relatively long periods of time. The point was to see whether the nature of a bank's business was more closely associated with its language of operations or with its size. Pearson correlations (r) were computed, testing for the impact of each independent variable, with the role of the other variable taken into account.[4] For instance, in order to know whether language was more closely related than size to the percentage of a bank's liabilities coming from sharehol-ders' funds between 1857 and 1925, two correlations had to be calculated. By computing the relationship between language and the dependence upon shareholders's funds, one gained a very weak correlation ($r = -.02$) upon controlling for the impact of the size the bank. In this calculation English banks were given the value of 'o' and French banks that of '1.' Accordingly, a slightly negative correlation meant that shareholders' funds made up a slightly greater percentage of total liabilities for the English banks than for the French ones, once one controlled for the bank's size. By contrast, a relatively strong relationship ($r = -.40$) was found by calculating the link between a bank's total assets and the percentage of its funds coming from its paid capital, with the negligible impact of language taken into account. In this last case, the smaller the bank the more likely it was to have been dependent upon funds from the sale of its stock.

This statistical series also includes three essential pieces of information, one which the *Canada Gazette* never reported and two which it only began to publish in 1880. It was necessary to look to the annual reports of all of Quebec's banks in order to come up with their net profits for the entire period. Most of the banks published these reports in newspapers or in business journals, but others such as the Banque du Peuple and the Banque de St-Jean refused to be so obliging over long periods of time. Whenever the data were available, however, the net profits were calculated as a percentage of the bank's paid capital to arrive at a common gauge of bank profitability that was the standard of the time. Based upon this percentage, the French banks, either individually or collectively, could be compared with other Quebec institutions. In addition, the dividends and reserve funds of these banks could be compared after collecting data for the period prior to 1880. When annual reports were not available, it was possible to find information regarding dividend payments in the stock quotations in the daily press. For the size of a bank's reserve, one was dependent once again upon annual reports. Once this information was secured, the reserve was seen as a percentage of paid capital as was the custom of the time.

With the last pieces of information included, this statistical series contains data such as are noted in table A.1 for one bank in one year.

II DATA REGARDING SHAREHOLDERS, 1871–1921

Information regarding the identity of bank shareholders came from the lists produced in Canadian *Sessional Papers* beginning in

TABLE A.1
Banque Nationale, 1861

Liabilities		Assets	
Paid capital	$351,219	Coin & bullion	$174,023
Notes in circulation	203,028	Government securities	36,000
Balance due other banks	0	Notes of other banks	25,833
Deposits not bearing		Due to other banks	53,707
interest	164,361	Notes & bills	
Deposits bearing		discounted	554,115
interest	116,931	Other assets	5,214
Total liabilities	$835,539	Total assets	$848,262
	Net profits	$32,030	
	Last dividend	8%	

1857 and continuing until 1917. After 1917 publication of this information ended, but the lists can be secured through the Public Archives.[5] Even the pre-1917 lists were not always available when it was arbitrarily decided that the information should be retained only for members of Parliament. In still other years, particularly in the pre-Confederation period and for some time after 1867, even when the lists were published they did not always contain information regarding all of the banks. As was the case with the *Canada Gazette* data, complete coverage was only achieved by around 1890.

Special attention was paid to the shareholders of Canada's banks for the census years from 1871 to 1921. Census years were selected for reasons that are beyond the purposes of this study, but in any event analysing these lists for all banks once per decade was all that could realistically be done, given the large number of shareholders that were listed. In 1871 there were over 14,000 names included, and the figure steadily increased to nearly 50,000 by 1921. With minor exceptions all of Canada's banks were included in the information for the six years singled out for analysis. In 1871 this was only achieved by employing lists published between 1871 and 1875, while for 1881 it was necessary to use information published between 1881 and 1884.

For each individual listed for each bank, four pieces of information were retained: the language of the shareholder, whether it was an individual or a corporate investor, the shareholder's place of residence, and the value of the investment. The issue of language was determined on the basis of the shareholder's name, which is admittedly a risky business. There were simply too many cases to allow further examination to see whether a Daniel Johnson was French or English. The alternative to adopting this approach would have been the abandonment of any attempt to judge the role of ethnicity in influencing investment in bank stock. Given the clear-cut distinctions that emerged between French and English investors, the impact of a few mistaken decisions regarding the language of a shareholder would not have altered the conclusions. However, to limit the number of such errors, when there was the least amount of doubt the shareholder was included in a category for borderline cases. In addition, the unpublished lists of shareholders for 1921 also included information regarding the occupation of each investor. Accordingly, the following information was available for one Banque Provinciale shareholder in 1921:

Name: Paul André
Occupation: Merchant
Residence: Ste-Lucie de Doncaster, Quebec
Value of Investment: $1,000

III   DIRECTORS OF THE QUEBEC BANKS,
1817–1925

References to the backgrounds of bank directors are based upon data collected regarding the men (there were no women) who sat on the boards of the Quebec banks between 1817 (the year of the establishment of the Bank of Montreal) and 1925. In all there were 765 directors, whose backgrounds had to be unearthed from a variety of biographical dictionaries, newspapers, city directories, and bank documents.[6] Information was collected on the date and place of birth of the shareholder, his ethnicity, his religion, his principal occupation, and his other business associations. For the purposes of this study, however, two pieces of information were retained for analysis. In terms of the ethnicity of the director, the major question was whether he was French or English, with the latter category including a variety of non-francophone possibilities. Where the name did not clearly indicate ethnicity, further research was carried out. For instance, a little digging indicated the Joseph-Marcellin *Wilson* was raised and educated in a francophone milieu.

The second type of information regarding each director that was retained for detailed analysis pertained to his principal occupation. It was not always easy to determine the primary occupation for men who were involved with numerous pursuits and who served as directors for long periods of time. Their occupations were sometimes known for years during which they were not leading a bank, while in other cases, even if their principal occupation could be determined at any one point in time, it changed during the course of their directorship. In spite of these problems, it was still possible to establish with confidence the principal occupations of 88% of the directors.

Once established, the occupation of each man was fitted into one of several categories based upon a classification scheme that considered each occupation according to its function (and not necessarily its status) within the economy.[7] Over 80% of the directors about whom the principal occupation was known could be fitted into one of four categories: professional men, merchants, manufacturers, and financiers.

IV BRANCHES OF CANADIAN BANKS, 1871 – 1921

Information was collected regarding the location of every branch or subagency of a chartered bank, as well as each caisse populaire, for the census years from 1871 to 1921. The data regarding the banks were culled from two sources, the *Banker's Almanac* for 1871, 1881, and 1891 and the *Rand-McNally Banker's Directory* thereafter. The caisse populaire information came from the *Annuaire du Québec*. No reliable lists were available prior to 1871, and the census years were chosen so that data regarding the population and the number of people of French origin in each community might be collected. Accordingly, using the directories and the census data, one could discover that the only bank in the Quebec town of Nicolet in 1901 was a branch of the Banque Nationale. The town had a population of 2,210, and 2,180 of these people were of French origin. As more than 75% of its population had a French background, Nicolet was the sort of town that is referred to in the text as an 'overwhelmingly French community.'

Notes

ABBREVIATIONS

PAC   Public Archives of Canada
BNC   Archives of the Banque Nationale du Canada
ANQ   Archives Nationales du Québec (Quebec City)
ANQM   Archives Nationales du Québec (Montreal)
PANS   Public Archives of Nova Scotia
CBA   Archives of the Canadian Bankers' Association
BNS   Bank of Nova Scotia Archives

PREFACE

1 Gerald Tulchinsky, *The River Barons* (Toronto 1977).
2 Paul-André Linteau, *Maisonneuve ou comment des promoteurs fabriquent une ville* (Montreal 1981).
3 See, for instance, *Banque Canadienne Nationale, 1874–1974* (n.p., n.d.), or R.S. Greenfield, 'La Banque du Peuple, 1835–1871, and Its Failure, 1895,' MA thesis, McGill University 1968.
4 Tom Naylor, *History of Canadian Business, 1867–1914* (Toronto 1975).
5 R.M. Breckenridge, *The Canadian Banking System 1817–1890* (Toronto 1894), 40.
6 Adam Shortt, 'The Banking System in Canada,' in *Canada and Its Provinces*, x (Toronto 1914).
7 Naylor, I, 135.
8 T. Solowij, 'Développement des Banques Canadiennes-françaises,' *Actualité Économique*, xxv (1949), 3–10; *Banque Canadienne Nationale, 1874–1974*; Greenfield, 'La Banque du Peuple'; Laurent Lapointe, 'La formation de la Banque de St-Hyacinthe et le développement économique régional (1850–1875),' MA thesis, Université de Montréal 1976; Lapointe's doctoral dissertation on the same bank is nearing completion at the moment.

CHAPTER ONE

1 Such a view was put forward by Michel Brunet, 'Trois dominantes de la pensée canadienne-française,' in *La présence anglaise et les Canadiens* (Montreal 1958), 113–66.

2 'Une Institution Nationale: La Banque du Peuple,' *La Revue Canadienne*, XXI (1895), 94.

3 Throughout this study 'savings deposits' will refer to the deposits which could only be withdrawn on a fixed day or after giving notice to the bank. 'Total deposits' will refer to the total of these savings deposits and other funds in current accounts which could be withdrawn on demand. This and all subsequent information in the text regarding assets, liabilities, profits, and dividends come from data which are discussed at length in appendix I.

4 H.M.P. Eckhardt, *A Rational Banking System* (New York 1911), 82. William Marr and Donald Paterson contradict Eckhardt's position by asserting in their *Canada: An Economic History* (Toronto 1980) that there is no proof that the banks moved 'funds from slow growing to fast growing regions' (476). Statistical support for Eckhardt's position can be found in J.D. Frost, 'The Nationalization of the Bank of Nova Scotia,' *Acadiensis*, III (Autumn 1982), 3–38 and Terrence Fay, 'Generation of Assets and Urban-Industrial Development: Winnipeg and Minneapolis, 1876–1925,' paper presented at Canadian-American Urban History Conference, University of Guelph, 1982.

5 Eckhardt, 'Distribution of Canada's Banking Facilities,' *Journal of Canadian Bankers' Association* (JCBA), XX (1912–13), 91–115.

6 See, for instance, Shirley Donald Southworth and John M. Chapman, *Banking Facilities for Bankless Towns* (New York 1941).

7 This and all subsequent references to bank branches are derived from data that are discussed in appendix IV.

8 JCBA, XXX, (1922), 262.

9 *Le Courrier de St-Hyacinthe*, 1 May 1857. The issue of the anti-industrial biases of Canada's banks is raised in Naylor's *History of Canadian Business*. Naylor's view has been contradicted by several writers, including Frost in his 'Nationalization of the Bank of Nova Scotia.'

10 For instance, among all of Canada's banks in 1921, those with total assets of $1 to $5 million declared a dividend of 7%, those with between $10 and $25 million 8%, between $25 and $100 million 11.3%, and more than $100 million 12.2%. Once one controls for size, there is scarcely any difference between French and English banks.

11 The figure of 75% is admittedly arbitrary and is used to highlight the position of towns with overwhelmingly French populations. Similar results were also received using 90%.

12 Ronald Rudin, 'The Development of Four Quebec Towns, 1840–1914,' PH D thesis, York University 1976, 256.

13 Ibid., 13.

14 PAC, Bank of Montreal papers (BM), Merchants' Bank directors' minutes, 15 September 1880.
15 Canada, Parliament, House of Commons, *Debates*, 8th Parl., 4th sess., 1 (1899): 3302.
16 PAC, BM, Merchants' Bank annual report, 9 June 1896.
17 André Raynauld, *Croissance et structures économiques de la province de Québec* (Quebec 1961), 590.
18 Paul-André Linteau, René Durocher and Jean-Claude Robert, *Histoire du Québec contemporain* (Montreal 1979), 374.
19 ANQM, Banque de St-Hyacinthe collection, box 52, balance sheet for 23 January 1908.
20 BNC, Banque Provinciale directors' minutes, 26 June–3 July 1908.
21 PAC, Sir Lomer Gouin papers, MG 27 III B4, vol. 43, Bank of Montreal to Gouin, 10 April 1923.
22 *Le Prix Courant*, 8 February 1889.
23 BM, Merchants' Bank directors' minutes, 30 July 1879. The name of the client has been withheld at the request of the Bank of Montreal.
24 BNC, Banque Jacques-Cartier directors' minutes, 19 February 1897.
25 BNS, Fyshe letters, Fyshe to Macleod, 7 July 1888.
26 Ibid., general manager to board of directors, 6 February 1907.
27 Ibid., 6 September 1906.
28 The data employed in this study regarding bank shareholders are discussed in appendix II, while appendix III deals with the information pertaining to bank directors.
29 *Le Prix Courant*, 8 February 1889. A correspondent to the journal noted that if the English banks were going to provide unsatisfactory services, the only answer was to 'fonder des banques canadiennes-françaises.'
30 Ibid., 10 August 1888.
31 *La Revue Canadienne*, XXI (1895), 86.
32 Canada, Parliament, House of Commons, *Debates*, 8th Parl., 4th sess., 3 (1899): 8755.
33 *Le Moniteur du Commerce*, 29 June 1894.
34 See appendix II.
35 BNC, Banque Provinciale directors' minutes, 29 September 1916.
36 Ibid., 29 June 1923.
37 Quebec, Legislative Assembly, *Sessional Papers*, 1922. 'Report of the Standing Committee of Agriculture, Immigration and Colonization on the Opportuneness [sic] of Creating an Agricultural Credit.' Testimony of J.H. Fortier, p. 176.
38 BNC, 37-B-9, inspector's report, 5 October 1923.
39 *Annuaire du Québec*, 1922.
40 CBA, vol. 1000, report of the committee on branch banks, 14 November 1918.
41 BNC, 132-B-9, deposits at each office of the Banque Nationale, 30 April 1924.
42 *Monetary Times*, 6 August 1880.

CHAPTER TWO

1 See, for instance, José Igartua, 'A Change in Climate: The Conquest and the *Marchands* of Montreal,' Canadian Historical Association, *Historical Papers*, 1974, pp. 115–34.
2 Brunet, *La présence anglaise*; Donald Creighton, *Empire of the St. Lawrence* (Toronto 1956), 154.
3 See appendix III.
4 Creighton, 154.
5 Ibid.; Fernand Ouellet, *Histoire économique et sociale du Québec, 1760–1850* (Montreal 1971).
6 T.S. Brown, 'Montreal Fifty Years Ago,' *New Dominion Monthly*, v (1870), 125.
7 *La Revue Canadienne*, xxi (1895), 85.
8 John George Lambton Durham, *Report on the Affairs of British North America*, C.P. Lucas, ed. (New York 1970), II, 41–2.
9 Breckenridge, 40.
10 *Canada and Its Provinces*, IV, 630–1.
11 Tulchinsky, 18.
12 Naylor, I, 158–61.
13 Greenfield, 31.
14 T.S. Brown, 25.
15 Tulchinsky, 18.
16 *Journal of Commerce*, 5 March 1877.
17 BM, Bank of Montreal annual meeting, 7 June 1847.
18 The bank was also probably showing its conservative nature by paying dividends lower than those for other Quebec banks of its size during this period (see appendix I). However, the failure on the part of the bank to issue annual reports makes it impossible to know whether the low dividends were not simply a function of low profits.
19 See appendix II.
20 See appendix III.
21 Tulchinsky, 19.
22 In 1881 these two institutions held 4% of the total investment in Canadian banks. These were the only investors to hold more than 1% of the total.
23 BNC, Caisse d'Economie de Notre-Dame de Québec, annual report, 15 June 1856.
24 Olivier Robitaille, *Précis historique de la Caisse d'Economie de Notre-Dame de Québec*, (n.p. 1878), 168.
25 Ibid., 172–4; Auguste Bechard, *Histoire de la Banque Nationale* (Quebec 1878), 26.
26 In 1871, for instance, Banque Nationale profits stood at 9.5% and dividends at 7.5%. All banks of its size earned 10.9% and paid dividends of only 6.8%.
27 BNC, Banque Nationale directors' minutes, 5 May 1874.
28 Robitaille, 168.

29 *Monetary Times*, 1 January 1875.
30 *Le Pays*, 16 December 1870.
31 *Monetary Times*, 27 December 1872.
32 *Statutes of Canada*, 1873, c. 12.
33 Ibid., 1875, c. 59.
34 McCord Museum, Hale papers, letter from Edward Hale to P. McGill, 22 February 1836.
35 PAC, Provincial Secretary's correspondence, vol. 358, 15 October 1854.
36 That its major accounts were with English-speaking clients is evident from the bank's minute books, now held by the Canadian Imperial Bank of Commerce.
37 Kathleen Lord, 'Municipal and Industrial Development: Saint-Jean, Quebec, 1848–1914,' MA thesis, Concordia University 1981.
38 PAC, records of the Department of Finance, RG19, E2C, vol. 482, file 616-4, list of shareholders of the Banque de St-Jean, 25 July 1873.
39 Ibid., memo from John Langton, 25 October 1873.
40 Ibid., deposition by J.E. Molleur, 18 October 1909.
41 *Monetary Times*, 9 October 1874.
42 *Le Moniteur du Commerce*, 5 February 1892; PAC, RG19, vol. 482, file 616-4, deposition by A.H. Lapierre, 18 October 1909.
43 See Rudin, 'Development of Four Quebec Towns.
44 *Le Courrier de St-Hyacinthe*, 15 May 1855.
45 Ibid., 8 April 1862; for further information on this and other issues relating to the formation of the Banque de St-Hyacinthe, see Lapointe, 'La formation de la Banque de St-Hyacinthe.
46 *Le Courrier de St-Hyacinthe*, 4 March 1861.
47 Ibid., 31 December 1868.
48 Ibid., 1 April 1857.
49 Lapointe, 126.
50 Ibid., 162.
51 Canada, Legislative Assembly, *Journals*, 1841, p. 129.
52 Archives du Seminaire de Trois-Rivières, prospectus, 11 April 1857.
53 *Statutes of Canada*, 1873, c. 14.
54 *L'Ere Nouvelle*, 13 April 1857.
55 ANQ, Quebec Bank papers, 6.1, June 1873.
56 *Le Courrier de St-Hyacinthe*, 7 June 1873.
57 *Le Journal des Trois-Rivières*, 21 October 1872.
58 Linteau et al., *Histoire du Québec contemporain*, 171.
59 Ouellet, 595.
60 For instance, there was a moderately strong relationship ($r = -.42$) between the percentage of a bank's liabilities coming from shareholders' funds and the value of its total assets, with the impact of language taken into account. Upon controlling for the impact of the size of the bank, there was a much weaker relationship ($r = +.20$) between the language of a bank's operations

and its dependence upon shareholders' funds. This last relationship all but disappears when one removes the impact of the Banque du Peuple, which stood out from all Quebec banks in its dependence upon its capital. For a further explanation of these calculations, see appendix 1.

CHAPTER THREE

1 The other two French banks which operated during this period, the Banque de St-Jean and the Banque de St-Hyacinthe, will be discussed in chapter 4.
2 *Le Moniteur du Commerce*, 9 March 1888.
3 Ibid., 6 March 1885.
4 Canada, Parliament, Senate, *Debates*, 8th Parl., 4th sess., 1 (1899): 311.
5 *Le Moniteur du Commerce*, 9 March 1888.
6 Ibid., 11 March 1887.
7 *Le Prix Courant*, 7 March 1890.
8 *La Revue Canadienne*, XXI (1895), 91–2.
9 *Monetary Times*, 19 July 1895.
10 PAC, BM, Bank of Montreal correspondence with New York agents, vol. 2, letter from general manager, 12 July 1895.
11 H.M.P. Eckhardt, *Manual of Canadian Banking* (Toronto 1909), 54–6.
12 *Le Moniteur du Commerce*, 10 October 1895.
13 PAC, RG19, vol. 483, John Livingstone to Charles Tupper, 12 June 1897.
14 Ibid.; *Statutes of Canada*, 1897, c. 75.
15 *Le Moniteur du Commerce*, 2 December 1898.
16 PAC, RG19, vol. 483, Tarte to Fielding, 9 May 1899.
17 Canada, Parliament, House of Commons, *Debates*, 8th Parl., 4th sess., 1 (1899): 3302.
18 *Statutes of Canada*, 1899, c. 123; PAC, RG19, vol. 483, memo dated 10 July 1908.
19 *Monetary Times*, 11 October 1896, 20 March 1896; RG19, vol. 483, f. 616-11, report to Senate, 21 April 1899.
20 *Monetary Times*, 10 November 1876.
21 These figures were later shown to have underestimated the bank's bad debts.
22 *La Patrie*, 8 August 1879.
23 Ibid., 3 November 1879.
24 Ibid., 17 December 1879.
25 *Statutes of Canada*, 1880, c. 47.
26 *Montreal Gazette*, 17 January 1881.
27 PAC, RG19, vol. 3014, f. 928, petition by shareholders of the Banque Ville-Marie to the Governor General, 15 January 1881.
28 *Statutes of Canada*, 1881, c. 35.
29 *Le Prix Courant*, 12 July 1895.
30 PAC, RG19, vol. 483, memo by M. Hutchinson, 22 January 1900.
31 Canada, Parliament, House of Commons, *Debates*, 8th Parl., 4th sess., 3 (1899): 8755.

32 *Le Moniteur du Commerce*, 29 June 1894.
33 The bank claimed a paid capital of roughly $475,000 throughout the 1800s and 1890s, but approximately $100,000 of this amount was held by the bank as a result of its difficulties in the 1870s. The bank was only legally allowed to issue notes up to the value of capital held by the public, and this was the source of its problems with the finance ministry.
34 RG19, vol. 483, J. Courtney to G. Foster, 21 September 1892.
35 *Montreal Gazette*, 22 November 1899.
36 RG19, vol. 483, Courtney to Foster, 21 September 1892.
37 *Le Moniteur du Commerce*, 18 June 1891.
38 *La Presse*, 26 July 1899.
39 *Montreal Gazette*, 3 August 1899, reference to article from *Quebec Mercury*.
40 PAC, Laurier papers, p. 36206, anonymous letter to Laurier, 2 August 1899.
41 Ibid., 35987, petition from residents of Marieville to Laurier.
42 PANS, Fielding papers, vol. 433, Fielding to J.S. Briefly, 30 December 1899.
43 *Le Moniteur du Commerce*, 17 August 1900.
44 Ibid., 29 September 1905.
45 *Monetary Times*, 2 July 1875.
46 *La Minerve*, 1 September 1875.
47 *Monetary Times*, 3 November 1876.
48 For more detail regarding the bank's connection with this railway, see Brian Young, *Promoters and Politicians* (Toronto 1978), 81–2.
49 PAC, BM, Molson's Bank directors' minutes, 8 June 1875.
50 *Monetary Times*, 15 June 1875.
51 *Statutes of Canada*, 1877, c. 55.
52 Young, *Promoters and Politicians*, 81–2; Quebec, Legislative Assembly, *Sessional Papers*, 1876, paper no. 19; *Montreal Gazette*, 2 December 1876.
53 *Journal of Commerce*, 24 May 1878.
54 *Monetary Times*, 10 January 1879; BNC, Banque Jacques-Cartier (BJC) directors' minutes, 9 January 1879.
55 These stock quotations are taken from newspapers of the time. The quotations were presented as a percentage of the par value of the stock. In 1884, for instance, the stock was listed at 80% of the par value of $25, meaning that the bank's shares were trading at $20.
56 Linteau, *Maisonneuve*, 44.
57 BNC, BJC, annual report, 18 June 1879.
58 Ibid., 19 June 1895.
59 *Monetary Times*, 24 June 1898.
60 PAC, Laurier papers, p. 34816, Bienvenu to Laurier, 23 June 1899.
61 E.P. Neufeld, *The Financial System of Canada* (Toronto 1972), 117.
62 BNC, BJC directors' minutes, 29 May 1900.
63 *Le Prix Courant*, 13 October 1899.
64 BNC, box marked 'arrangements relatifs à la réorganisation,' memo to Bienvenu, 28 September 1899.

65 BNC, BJC directors' minutes, 7 December 1899.
66 Ibid., 7 December 1899, 21 December 1899, 19 March 1900.
67 BNC, Banque Nationale annual report, 18 May 1893.
68 *Le Prix Courant*, 31 May 1889.
69 *Le Moniteur du Commerce*, 31 May 1889.
70 PAC, RG19, vol. 3002, f. 255, petition dated 7 March 1883.
71 *Monetary Times*, 14 June 1895.
72 *Montreal Star*, 1 August 1899.
73 *Le Moniteur du Commerce*, 22 June 1900.
74 BNC, Banque d'Hochelaga directors' minutes, 26 May 1879.
75 Ibid., 11 March 1882.
76 Archives of the Archdiocese of Montreal, Bruchési to St-Charles, 26 June 1900.
77 *Le Moniteur du Commerce*, 22 June 1900.
78 The following correlations pertain to the affairs of Quebec-based banks between 1876 and 1900. For further details, see appendix I.

Selected aspects of bank operations	Correlation with language (controlling for size)	Correlation with total assets (controlling for language)
Percentage of liabilities from shareholders' funds	−.03	−.21
Percentage of assets tied up in current loans	−.06	−.31
Profits as percentage of paid capital	−.07	+.22

79 For the sources for this information, see appendix III.

CHAPTER FOUR

1 Lord, 'Municipal Aid and Industrial Development.'
2 Throughout this chapter, the profits of the Banque de St-Jean were calculated as a percentage of the *reported* paid capital. As was seen in chapter two, however, there is some question whether the reported value was the same as the real value of the paid capital.
3 *Le Moniteur du Commerce*, 17 February 1888.
4 PAC, RG19, vol. 3092, f. 6036, memo by J. Courtney 22 September 1893.
5 Canada, Parliament, House of Commons, *Debates*, 8th parl., 4th sess., 1 (1899): 3302.

6 *Le Canada Français*, 8 October 1975.

7 *Monetary Times*, 2 May 1908.

8 *Le Canada Français*, 9 October 1975, 15 October 1975.

9 PAC, RG19, vol. 482, F.W. Hibbard to deputy minister, 20 June 1908.

10 *Le Moniteur du Commerce*, 1 May 1908.

11 ANQ, papers of the Ministry of Justice, vol. 260, f. 990.

12 *La Presse*, 15 May 1909.

13 Some shareholders tried to escape their double liability by claiming that the bank had never legally existed, owing to the dubious nature of its paid capital. See PAC, RG19, E2C, vol. 482, f. 616-4, petition by Alfred Lapierre, 18 October 1909.

14 One can find various figures regarding the final payment made to Banque de St-Jean depositors, but none of these exceed 30%.

15 The industrial figures for 1901 only include factories with five or more employees, so as to underestimate the growth during the 1890s. See Rudin, 'The Development of Four Quebec Towns.'

16 ANQM, Banque de St-Hyacinthe collection (BSTH), directors' minutes, 29 January 1878, 3 June 1881.

17 ANQM, BSTH, box 67, deed dated 31 March 1898.

18 *Le Courrier de St-Hyacinthe*, 23 February 1893.

19 ANQM, BSTH, box 67, agreement dated 12 December 1899.

20 Ibid., Cannon to Dessaulles, 6 September 1901.

21 Ibid., directors' minutes, 1 August 1902.

22 Ibid., box 68, suit filed by L.F. Morison, 17 July 1900.

23 *Report of the Exchequer Court of Canada*, XII (1909).

24 ANQM, BSTH, annual meeting, 15 December 1904.

25 CBA, vol. 1040, John Knight to W.T. White, 3 May 1913.

26 RG19, vol. 482, petition from residents of St-Marc and St-Charles, n.d.

27 ANQM, BSTH, 29 December 1902, 13 January 1905.

28 Ibid., box 66, Morin to Dessaulles, 9 February 1905.

29 Ibid., box 53, branch balances, June 1908.

30 Ibid., box 64, Edward Clouston to Dessaulles, 4 February 1903.

31 Ibid., directors' minutes, 1903–8.

32 CBA, vol. 1040, Knight to White, 3 May 1913.

33 Canada, Parliament, House of Commons, *Debates*, 12th parl., 2nd sess., 4 (1912–13): 10666.

34 Ibid., 10665.

35 Ibid., *Journals*, 12th Parl., 2nd sess. (1912–13), appendix II, 94–5, letter from D.R. Wilkie to W.T. White, 3 May 1913.

36 CBA, vol. 1040, Wilkie to White, 28 April 1913.

37 Ibid., Knight to Wilkie, 28 April 1913.

38 PAC, Gouin papers, vol. 43, Bank of Montreal to Gouin, 10 April 1923.

39 Canadian Imperial Bank of Commerce archives (CIBC), Eastern Townships Bank (ETB), directors' minutes, 15 September 1859.

40 CIBC, ETB, annual report, 1871.
41 Ibid., directors' minutes, 18 August 1880.
42 Ibid., 14 November 1899, 13 June 1895.
43 *Le Prix Courant*, 24 May 1894.
44 Cleyn and Tinker Company (Huntingdon, Quebec), Paton Manufacturing Company papers, vol. 3.
45 PAC, British American Land Company papers, vol. 3, pp. 667–9, letter from Heneker to Henry Paull, 26 June 1889.
46 *Sherbrooke Daily Record*, 17 June 1898.
47 CIBC, ETB, directors' minutes, 5 June 1899.
48 Ibid., 3 December 1902.
49 Ibid., based upon advances noted in course of 1909 in the bank's minute books.
50 Ibid., 29 May 1911.
51 Ibid., 7 June 1905.
52 Ibid., 5 December 1911. For further detail regarding the history of the ETB, see the author's 'Naissance et déclin d'une élite locale: la Banque des Cantons de l'Est,' *Revue d'histoire de l'Amerique française*, XXXVIII (1984), 165–179.

CHAPTER FIVE

1 See table 1.3.
2 *L'Action française*, VI (1921), 713–14.
3 Linteau et al., *Histoire du Québec contemporain*, 370–76.
4 BNC, Banque Provinciale, directors' minutes, 13 October 1922.
5 CBA, vol. 1040, Bienvenu to F.W. Taylor, 4 November 1922.
6 Ibid., executive council minute books, 7 March 1916.
7 Ibid., vol. 1040, committee on branches, n.d.; BNC, Banque Provinciale directors' minutes, 9 August 1918.
8 Controlling for the size of the bank, there was a correlation of +.16 between the language of a bank's operations and its profitability. A positive relationship meant that the French banks were more profitable. See appendix I.
9 BNC, Banque Provinciale annual assembly, 23 January 1901.
10 Ibid., directors' minutes, 29 August 1900.
11 Ibid., 20 April 1923.
12 Ibid., 14 February 1916.
13 Ibid., 8 January 1902.
14 Ibid., 30 January 1902, 13 March 1907, 4 May 1907.
15 Ibid., annual assembly, 26 January 1910.
16 PAC, RG19, vol. 817, investments of the Banque Provinciale as of 30 November 1923.
17 Ibid.
18 BNC, Banque Provinciale, annual assembly, 27 January 1904.
19 PAC, RG19, vol. 33358, f.17638, circular letter of 15 January 1909.

20 BNC, Banque Provinciale, directors' minutes, 27 March 1906.
21 *Le Moniteur du Commerce*, 13 July 1906.
22 CBA, vol. 1039, A.R. Biron to residents of Papineauville, 9 October 1922.
23 PAC, RG19, vol. 817, investments of the Banque Provinciale as of 30 November 1923.
24 Ibid.
25 Robert Bickerdike sat on the board from 1887 to 1911, and was followed by C.A. Smart (1911–13) and A.W. Bonner (1913–24).
26 BNS, letter from general manager to directors, 6 September 1906.
27 BNC, Béïque papers.
28 Ibid., Morrice to Béïque, 18 May 1897.
29 This information was derived from records kept by the Hochelaga's board of directors regarding each loan discussed. This series, which is housed in the BNC archives and which begins in 1915, would appear to deal with even the smallest accounts. In any event, the largest accounts were certainly all included, and the calculations here deal with all accounts which exceeded $100,000 in the course of 1921.
30 Quebec, Legislative Assembly, *Sessional Papers*, 1922. 'Report of the Standing Committee of Agriculture, Immigration and Colonization on the Opportuneness [sic] of Creating an Agricultural Credit,' 214–15.
31 BNC, item 259, branch returns, 1915–50. This series provided data regarding the loans and deposits of each branch. The information employed here pertains to the situation at the close of 1921.
32 BNC, 37-B-10, inspector's report, 29 June 1922.
33 Ibid., 37-B-9, inspector's report, 5 October 1923; based upon a sample of every second directors' meeting in the course of 1921, 62.5% of the value of advances made at Lafléche went to English-speakers.
34 BNC, Banque Nationale, Montmagny letterbook, Prudent Vallée to Napoléon Lavoie, 18 September 1915.
35 Yves Roby, *Alphonse Desjardins et les Caisses Populaires* (Ottawa 1964), 107.
36 BNC, 132-B-9, deposits at each office of the Banque Nationale, 30 April 1924.
37 Archives de la Fédération des Caisses Populaires (Lévis), 21: 2.1-1-7.25, Desjardins to H. Bourassa, 4 December 1914.
38 Ibid., 21: 2.1-10.5, Desjardins to J.V. Rochette, 21 October 1914; BNC, Banque Nationale, annual assembly, 9 June 1915.
39 This calculation is based upon *Canada Gazette* data (see appendix I) adjusted to account for misrepresentations noted in the CBA's audit of the bank in early 1922. See CBA, vol. 1001, W. Bog to F.W. Taylor, 19 January 1922.
40 Eckhardt, *Manual of Canadian Banking*, 54.
41 BNC, 132-B-9, Banque Nationale deposits, 30 April 1924.
42 BNC, Compagnie Manufacturière de Montmagny, minute books, 12 March 1908.
43 BNC, Montmagny letterbooks, 28 August 1911.
44 Ibid., 9 April 1913.

45 *Quebec Gazette*, 2 November 1912.
46 PAC, Imperial Munitions Board papers, MG28 190, ledger of contracts.
47 BNC, 132-B-9, Lavoie to Paquet, 3 February 1917.
48 Ibid., 'Remarques de M.N. Lavoie,' 19 February 1924.
49 There are various estimates regarding the Machine Agricole debt at the start
   of 1921. All parties are agreed that $1.5 million was added to the debt during
   1921. Taking this into account, the $2.3 million figure came from CBA, vol.
   1001, W. Bog to F.W. Taylor, 19 January 1922. A figure of nearly $3 million
   can be gained from PAC, Gouin papers, vol. 33, f. 75, Lavoie to Gouin, 21
   December 1921.
50 CBA, vol. 1001, Bog to Taylor, 19 January 1922.
51 BNC, 132-B-9, address by G.E. Amyot to Machine Agricole bondholders, n.d.
52 PAC, Gouin papers, vol. 33, f. 75, speech by Lavoie to Banque Nationale
   annual assembly, 14 June 1922.
53 Neufeld, 118.
54 This was one of the few cases in this study in which language played a more
   important role than size in influencing bank operations. There was a very
   weak relationship ($r = -.09$) between the size of the bank and the percentage
   of its liabilities derived from savings deposits (controlling for the impact of
   language). By contrast, there was a correlation of $+.24$ between this percentage and the language of the bank (controlling for size). See appendix I.
55 Robert Sweeny, *A Guide to the History and Records of Selected Montreal
   Businesses Before 1947* (Montreal 1978), 37.
56 Ibid., 221.

CHAPTER SIX

1 An earlier version of many of the arguments presented in this chapter can be
   found in my 'A Bank Merger Unlike the Others: The Establishment of the
   Banque Canadienne Nationale,' *Canadian Historical Review*, LXI (1980), 191–
   212. I appreciate the co-operation of the *CHR* in allowing me to employ here
   some of the material presented in that article.
2 BNC, Banque Nationale, directors' minutes, 30 August 1875; *Montreal Star*, 8
   December 1879.
3 *Le Moniteur du Commerce*, 5 October 1883.
4 Ibid., 1 September 1905.
5 *Le Devoir*, 17 January 1922.
6 *L'Action Française*, VI (1921), 713–14.
7 BNC, 132-B-9, 'Remarques de Lavoie,' 19 February 1924.
8 Ibid., Montmagny letterbooks, 25 January 1922.
9 *La Minerve*, 26 April 1924.
10 PAC, Gouin papers, vol. 33, f. 75, Lavoie to Gouin, 21 December 1921.
11 Ibid.
12 Ibid.; PANS, Fielding papers, vol. 493, Fielding to Lavoie, 3 January 1922.

13 CBA, vol. 1001, Bog to Taylor, 19 January 1922.
14 Ibid.
15 Ibid.
16 Ibid.
17 PAC, Gouin papers, vol. 39, f. 122, Leman to Taylor, 18 January 1922.
18 Ibid.
19 Ibid., Bienvenu to Taylor, 21 January 1922.
20 *Financial Post*, 27 January 1922.
21 BNC, Banque Nationale, annual assembly, 14 June 1922.
22 Ibid.
23 Ibid., directors' minutes, 8 August 1922; PAC, Gouin papers, vol. 25, Amyot to Gouin, 22 March 1922, 5 April 1922, 11 April 1922.
24 PANS, Fielding papers, vol. 493, Fielding to Taylor, 3 February 1922.
25 PAC, Gouin papers, vol. 25, Amyot to Gouin, 5 April 1922; Gouin to Amyot, 12 April 1922.
26 BNC, Banque Nationale, annual assembly, 13 June 1923.
27 Ibid., 132-B-9, circular from Ligue de protection des épargnes de la province de Québec, 26 July 1923.
28 PAC, Gouin papers, vol. 36, f. 98, Paquet to Gouin, 26 January 1922.
29 BNC, Montmagny letterbooks, 15 March 1922.
30 Ibid., 28 October 1922.
31 Ibid., 28 October to 5 December 1922.
32 Ibid., Banque Nationale, employee records.
33 PANS, Fielding papers, vol. 533, f. 131, J.L. Laferrière to Fielding, 2 November 1923.
34 PAC, RG19, vol. 490, Amyot to Fielding, 28 November 1923.
35 Quebec, Legislative Assembly, *Journals*, 1924, pp. 77–84.
36 Statutes of Canada, 1925, c. 45.
37 *Monetary Times*, 25 January 1924.
38 Ibid.
39 *Financial Post*, 5 January 1924; *Financial Times*, 5 January 1924; *Le Devoir*, 23 January 1924.
40 *Le Soleil*, 3 January 1924.
41 *Monetary Times*, 25 January 1924.
42 BNC, 132-B-9, 'Rapport de l'Application des $15,000,000.'
43 *Monetary Times*, 25 January 1924.
44 *Le Devoir*, 21 January 1924.
45 Ibid.
46 Ibid.
47 Between 31 July and 30 November 1922, these loans increased from $294,627 to $716, 595.
48 *Le Devoir*, 23 January 1924.
49 *La Minerve*, 12 January 1924. The political implications of Taschereau's actions were pursued by the Conservatives in a number of by-elections in the fall. See my 'A Bank Merger Unlike the Others,' 210–11.

50 *Monetary Times*, 25 January 1922.
51 Ibid.
52 BNC, Banque d'Hochelaga, shareholders' meeting, 21 February 1924.
53 BNC, Banque Provinciale, annual assembly, 6 February 1924.
54 PAC, Gouin papers, vol. 26, Bienvenu to Gouin, 2 January 1924; Robert Rumilly, *Histoire de la province de Québec* (Montreal 1940–69), XXVII, 104.
55 BNC, Banque d'Hochelaga, annual assembly, 15 January 1925.
56 Anatole Vanier, 'La Ligue d'Action française et la Banque d'Hochelaga, L'Action française, XII (1924), 62.
57 BNC, 132-B-9, Banque d'Hochelaga, auditor's reports, November 1922; November 1923.
58 BNC, Banque d'Hochelaga, directors' decisions regarding loans, 1 January to 31 December 1923.
59 PAC, BM, Molson's Bank, directors' minutes, 30 October 1923; 26 February 1924; 20 June 1924; 3 November 1924; 23 January 1925.
60 PAC, Meighen papers, vol. 61, p. 34378, circular from Ligue de protection des épargnes de la province de Québec, 15 January 1925.
61 BNC, Banque d'Hochelaga, shareholders' meetings, 21 February 1924.
62 PAC, Meighen papers, pp. 33450–4, circular from Ligue de protection, 23 March 1925.
63 BNC, Banque Provinciale, directors' minutes, 15 January 1924.
64 Ibid., 132-B-9, Lavoie to Bienvenu, 9 February 1924.
65 ANQ, Taschereau papers, Vaillancourt to Laporte, 12 March 1924.
66 BNC, Banque Provinciale, directors' minutes, 3 July 1925 to 5 May 1926.

CHAPTER SEVEN

1 Prior to Naylor's work there was little serious archival research into the history of the operations of Canada's banks. In particular, as a result of Naylor's assertions regarding the regional impact of the banking system, interesting studies have emerged pertaining to the prairies and the Maritimes. See Fay, 'Generation of Assets and Urban Industrial Development,' and Frost, 'The "Nationalization" of the Bank of Nova Scotia.'
2 Despite Naylor's claims that the American system allowed capital to remain in the community where it originated, there is evidence that correspondent banking permitted the same flow of funds evident in the Canadian system of branch banking. See John James, *Capital Markets in Postbellum America* (Princeton 1978).
3 This was particularly clear in the operations of the Banque d'Hochelaga in the first decades of the 1900s. See table 5.2
4 BNC, item 259, branch returns, 1915–50.
5 Roby, 123–38.
6 Bernard Vigod, 'Response to Economic and Social Change in Quebec: The Provincial Administration of Louis-Alexandre Taschereau,' PH D thesis, Queen's University 1974, p. 331.

7 Brian Young, *George-Etienne Cartier* (Montreal 1981).
8 The following correlations were calculated for the period from 1857 to 1925. For an explanation of the calculations, see appendix I.

Selected aspects of bank operations	Correlation with language (controlling for size)	Correlation with total assets (controlling for language)
Profits (calculated as percentage of paid capital)	+.01	+.44
Dividends	−.32	+.51
Reserve fund (calculated as percentage of paid capital)	−.19	+.51
Percentage of total liabilities coming from shareholders' funds	−.02	−.40
Percentage of total assets tied up in current loans	−.001	−.21

9 For a review of this literature, see René Durocher and Paul-André Linteau, eds., *Le retard du Québec et l'infériorité économique des Canadiens français* (Montreal 1971).

APPENDICES

1 C.A. Curtis, 'Statistics of Banking,' in *Statistical Contributions to Canadian Economic History* (Toronto 1931).
2 The Banque de St-Jean situation is discussed in chapter 4, while the Ville-Marie misrepresentations are dealt with in chapter 3.
3 See chapter 6.
4 For an explanation of this statistical measure, see Hubert Blalock, *Social Statistics* (New York 1972); or G.V. Glass and J.C. Stanley, *Statistical Methods in Education and Psychology* (Englewood Cliffs, New Jersey 1970).
5 PAC, RG14, D2, vols. 1038–9.
6 *Lovell's Montreal Directory* yielded considerable information, as did the various biographical dictionaries, most of which are listed in Dorothy Ryder, comp., *Canadian Reference Sources* (Toronto 1981).
7 My thanks to Bettina Bradbury for providing me with her occupational classification scheme. For a discussion of the problems involved in choosing the appropriate scheme, see Michael Katz, 'Occupational Classification in History,' *Journal of Interdisciplinary History*, III (1972), 63–88.

Bibliography

PRIMARY SOURCES

1. Manuscript Collections

Archives Nationales du Québec (Quebec City)
  Ministry of Justice Papers
  Quebec Bank Papers
  Taschereau Papers
Archives Nationales du Québec (Montreal)
  Banque de St-Hyacinthe Collection
Banque Nationale du Canada Archives
  Banque d'Hochelaga, Branch Returns, 1915–25 (item 259)
  Banque d'Hochelaga, Directors' Decisions Regarding Loans,
    1915–25
  Banque d'Hochelaga, Inspectors' Reports (37–B-9 to 12)
  Banque Nationale, Montmagny Letterbooks, 1899–1922
  Caisse d'Economie de Notre-Dame de Québec, Minute Books
  Compagnie Manufacturière de Montmagny, Minute Books
  Directors' Minutes: Banque d'Hochelaga, Banque Jacques-
    Cartier, Banque Nationale, Banque Provinciale
  Documents relating to merger of Banque d'Hochelaga and
    Banque Nationale (132-B-9)
  Papers of F.L. Béïque

Bank of Nova Scotia Archives
  Branch Ledgers
  Letters from general manager to directors, 1900–20
Canadian Bankers' Association Archives
  Correspondence and Reports
Canadian Imperial Bank of Commerce Archives
  Canadian Bank of Commerce Directors' Minutes, 1911–12
  Eastern Townships Bank, Directors' Minutes, 1859–1912
Fédération des Caisses Populaires Archives (Lévis)
  Correspondence of Alphonse Desjardins
Public Archives of Canada
  Bank of Montreal Collection
  Borden Papers
  Department of Finance Papers
  Gouin Papers
  Imperial Munitions Board Papers
  King Papers
  Laurier Papers
  Macdonald Papers
  Meighen Papers
  Treasury Board Papers
  White Papers
Public Archives of Nova Scotia
  Fielding Papers

2. *Newspapers and Journals*

  Financial Post, 1907–25
  Financial Times, 1912–25
  Journal of the Canadian Bankers' Association, 1893–1925
  Journal of Commerce, 1875–1925
  Monetary Times, 1867–1925
  Le Moniteur du Commerce, 1881–1925
  Le Prix Courant, 1887–1925

3. Printed Primary Sources

A. Government Documents
   Canada. *Canada Gazette*, 1857–1925
   Canada. *Census of Canada*, 1871–1921
   Canada. Parliament. House of Commons. *Debates*, 1867–1925
   Canada. Parliament. House of Commons. *Journals*, 12th Parl.,
     2nd sess., app. II (1912–13)
   Canada. Parliament. *Sessional Papers*, 1857–1917. Lists of the
     shareholders of the chartered banks
   Canada. *Statutes of Canada*, 1840–1925
   Quebec. Legislative Assembly. *Sessional Papers, 1876*. Paper
     no. 19; 1922, 'Report of the Standing Committee on Agricul-
     ture'

B. Other Printed Materials
   Bankers' Almanac and Register. New York 1881–91
   Bechard, Auguste. *Histoire de la Banque Nationale*. Quebec 1878
   Eastern Townships Bank. *Charter and Annual Reports, 1859–
     1912*. Sherbrooke 1912
   Houston, W.R., comp. *Annual Financial Review*. Toronto 1901–
     25
   Rand-McNally Bankers' Directory. Chicago 1901–21
   Robitaille, Olivier. *Précis historique de la Caisse d'Economie de
     Notre-Dame de Québec*. n.p. 1878

SECONDARY SOURCES

1. Books
Banque Canadienne Nationale, 1874–1974, n.p., n.d.
Beckhart, B.H. *The Banking System of Canada*. New York 1929
Bliss, Michael *A Canadian Millionaire: The Life and Business Times
   of Sir Joseph Flavelle*. Toronto 1978
– *A Living Profit*. Toronto 1974
Breckenridge, R.M. *The Canadian Banking System, 1817–1890*.
   Toronto 1894

Brunet, Michel *La présence anglaise et les canadiens*. Montreal, 1958

Cameron, Rondo, ed. *Banking and Economic Development*. New York 1972

– *Banking in the Early Stages of Industrialization*. New York 1967

Chapman, John M., and Ray Westfall *Branch Banking*. New York 1917

Creighton, Donald *The Empire of the St. Lawrence*. Toronto 1956

Davis, Lance, and D.C. North *Institutional Change and American Economic Growth*. London 1971

Denison, Merrill *Canada's First Bank*. Toronto 1966

Durocher, René, and Paul-André Linteau, eds. *Le retard du Québec et l'infériorité économique des Canadiens-français*. Montreal 1971

Eckhardt, H.M.P. *Manual of Canadian Banking*. Toronto 1909

– *A Rational Banking System*. New York 1911

Gerschenkron, Alexander *Economic Backwardness in Historical Perspective*. Cambridge 1962

Hamelin, Jean, and Yves Roby *Histoire économique du Québec, 1851–1896*. Montreal 1971

Hull, Walter *Practical problems in Banking and Currency*. New York 1907

James, John *Capital Markets in Postbellum America*. Princeton 1978

Jamieson, A.B. *Chartered Banking in Canada*. Toronto 1957

Johnson, Joseph French *The Canadian Banking System*. Washington 1910

Knight, John, comp. *Canadian Banking Practice*. Toronto 1912

Landes, David *Bankers and Pashas*. New York 1969

Linteau, Paul-André *Maisonneuve ou comment des promoteurs fabriquent une ville*. Montreal 1981

Linteau, Paul-André, René Durocher, and Jean-Claude Robert *Histoire du Québec contemporain*. Montreal 1979

Marr, William, and Donald Paterson *Canada: An Economic History*. Toronto 1980

Moreau, François *Le capital financier québécois*. Montreal 1981

Naylor, Tom *History of Canadian Business*. 2 vols. Toronto 1975

Neufeld, E.P. *The Financial System of Canada*. Toronto 1972
Ouellet, Fernand *Histoire économique et sociale du Québec*. Montreal 1971
Patterson, E.L. *Canadian Banking*. Toronto 1932
Pomfret, Richard *The Economic Development of Canada*. Toronto 1981
Raynauld, André *Croissance et structures économiques de la province du Québec*. Quebec 1961
Roby, Yves *Alphonse Desjardins et les Caisses Populaires*. Ottawa 1964
– *Les Québécois et les investissements américains*. Quebec 1976
Ross, Victor *A History of the Canadian Bank of Commerce*. Toronto 1920
Ryan, William *The Clergy and Economic Growth in Quebec*. Quebec 1966
Ryba, André *Le rôle du secteur financier dans le développement économique du Québec*. Montreal 1974
Southworth, Shirley Donald, and John M. Chapman *Banking Facilities for Bankless Towns*. New York 1941
Sweeney, Robert *A Guide to the History and Records of Selected Montreal Businesses Before 1947* Montreal 1978
Tremblay, Rodrique *L'Economie québécoise*. Montreal 1976
Tulchinsky, Gerald *The River Barons*. Toronto 1977
United States National Monetary Commission *Interviews on the Banking and Currency Systems of Canada*. Washington 1910
Young, Brian *George-Etienne Cartier*. Montreal 1981
– *Promoters and Politicians*. Toronto 1978

2. *Articles*
Conzen, Michael 'Capital Flows and the Developing Urban Hierarchy: State Bank Capital in Wisconsin, 1854–1895,' *Economic Geography*, LI (1975), 321–38.
Curtis, C.A. 'Statistics of Banking,' in *Statistical Contribution to Canadian Economic History*. Toronto 1931
Deane, Phyllis 'The Role of Capital in the Industrial Revolution,' *Explorations in Economic History*, x (1973), 349–64
Drummond, Ian 'Canadian Life Assurance Companies and the

Capital Market, 1890–1914,' *Canadian Journal of Economics and Political Science*, XXVIII (1962), 202–24
- Review of R.T. Naylor, '*History of Canadian Business*,' *Canadian Historical Review*, LIX (1978), 90–3
Frost, J.D. 'The "Nationalization" of the Bank of Nova Scotia, *Acadiensis*, III (1982), 3–38
Hague, George 'The Banking System of Canada,' in *Canadian Economics*. Montreal 1885
Hammond, Bray 'Banking in Canada Before Confederation,' in W.T. Easterbrook and M.H. Waltsins, eds., *Approaches to Canadian Economic History*. Toronto 1967
Igartua, José 'A Change in Climate: The Conquest and the *Marchands* of Montreal.' Canadian Historical Association, *Historical Papers*, 1974, pp. 115–34
'Une Institution Nationale: La Banque du Peuple,' *Revue Canadienne*, XXI (1895), 82–97
Linteau, Paul-André 'Quelques réflexions autour de la bourgeoisie québécoise, 1850–1914,' *Revue d'histoire de l'Amérique française*, XXX (1976), 55–66
Liversay, H.C., and Glenn Porter 'The Financial Role of Merchants in the Development of United States Manufacturing, 1815–60,' *Explorations in Economic History*, IX (1971), 63–88
Macdonald, Larry 'Merchants against Industry: An Idea and Its Origins,' *Canadian Historical Review*, LVI (1975), 263–81
McCalla, Douglas 'Tom Naylor's *A History of Canadian Business*: A Comment,' Canadian Historical Association, *Historical Papers*, 1976, pp. 249–54
Pollard, Sidney 'Fixed Capital in the Industrial Revolution in Britain,' *Journal of Economic History*, XXIV (1964), 299–314
Rudin, Ronald 'A Bank Merger Unlike the Others: The Establishment of the Banque Canadienne Nationale,' *Canadian Historical Review*, LXI (1980), 191–212
Sylla, Richard 'American Banking and Growth in the Nineteenth Century,' *Explorations in Economic History*, IX (1971–2), 197–228
Shortt, Adam 'The Banking System in Canada,' in *Canada and Its Provinces*. Toronto 1914

Solowij, T. 'Développement des banques canadiennes-françaises,' *Actualité Economique*, xxv (1949), 3–10.

3. *Unpublished Material*

Code, William Robert 'The Spatial Dynamics of Financial Intermediaries. An Interpretation of the Distribution of Financial Decision-Making in Canada.' PH D thesis, University of California 1971.

Diamond, Sheldon 'An Analysis of the Canadian Bank of Commerce Directorate, 1869–1928.' MA thesis, University of Western Ontario 1978.

Fay, Terence 'Generation of Assets and Urban-Industrial Development: Winnipeg and Minneapolis, 1876–1926.' Paper presented at Canadian-American Urban History Conference, University of Guelph 1982

Frost, J.D. 'Principles of Interest: The Bank of Nova Scotia and the Industrialization of the Maritimes, 1880–1910.' MA thesis, Queen's University 1978

Greenfield, R.S. 'La Banque du Peuple, 1835–1871, and Its Failure, 1895.' MA thesis, McGill University 1968

Lapointe, Laurent 'La Formation de la Banque de St-Hyacinthe et le développement économique régional.' MA thesis, Université de Montréal 1976

Lord, Kathleen 'Municipal Aid and Industrial Development: Saint-Jean, Quebec, 1848–1914.' MA thesis, Concordia University 1981

Rudin, Ronald 'The Development of Four Quebec Towns, 1840–1914.' PH D thesis, York University 1976.

Vigod, Bernard 'Response to Economic and Social Change in Quebec: The Provincial Administration of Louis-Alexandre Taschereau.' PH D thesis, Queen's University 1974

Index

Aird and Son 107
Alliance Nationale 117
Amyot, Georges-Elie 125–6, 128–30, 135
Archambault, Louis 57
Atkinson, Henry 33
Audette, Rodolphe 70, 110, 146

Bank Act 21, 61, 111
Bank of British North America 74, 120
Bank of Commerce 95
Bank of Montreal 3, 4, 16, 120, 138, 144; and Banque de St-Hyacinthe suspension 89–90; and Banque du Peuple 28, 51; branches 10–11, 14, 36, 43–4; and Eastern Townships Bank 95; establishment 23; and French directors 24
Bank of Nova Scotia 15
Banque Agricole 41
Banque Canadienne Nationale 6, 121, 131, 137

Banque des Marchands 31
Banque de St-Hyacinthe:
establishment 42–3;
operations 14, 78–80, 85–8;
suspension and liquidation 89–91
Banque de St-Jean 10, 152, 154;
establishment 37–40;
operations 13, 40, 78–83; suspension and liquidation 83–4
Banque des Trois-Rivières 43–4
Banque d'Hochelaga 10, 146; acquisition of Banque Nationale (see also Bill 3) 124–5, 136–9; branches 72, 108, 139, 142; change of name 137; directors 110; and English capital 20, 108–9; and English clients 106; establishment 35; and French capital 104, 108–9; operations 47, 72–4, 105–9; and panic of 1899 67, 72; structure of assets and liabilities 72–3, 75, 102, 112, 133–4, 137–9

Banque du Peuple 3–4, 28, 75–6, 81, 131, 140, 146, 154; branches 13, 32, 49–50; and English capital 25, 29, 50; establishment 25–6; operations 28–9, 47–51; organization as *société en commandite* 27–9; suspension and liquidation 46, 51–5; treatment by historians 24

Banque Internationale 102

Banque Jacques-Cartier 75–6, 146; branches 65–6; and English capital 35, 64; establishment 34; and French clientele 15; operations 34, 64–6, 71; rumours of merger 120; reorganization 46, 66–9, 91; suspension of 1875 62–3

Banque Nationale 67, 75, 120, 121, 140, 146, 152; acquisition by Banque d'Hochelaga (*see* Bill 3); branches 70–1, 110–11, 128–9; competition with caisses populaires 19, 111–12; dependence on timber trade 69–71; directors 110; and English capital 33, 71; establishment 31–2; and French capital 32–3, 110; operations 33, 47, 69–72, 110–16, 122–30; reorganization of 1922 125–6; requests for federal government support 123–4, 126–7, 129; structure of assets and liabilities 102, 111–12, 133–4; subagencies 20, 112; and

Taschereau government 125–7, 130

Banque Provinciale 6, 146; branches 18–20, 100–1, 139; *commissaires-censeurs* 100; directors 102–5, 110; establishment 68–9; and French capital 100–1, 104; operations 99–105; structure of assets and liabilities 100–2, 112, 117, 137; subagencies 20; and takeover of Banque Nationale 124–5, 136–7

Banque St-Jean Baptiste 36, 56

Banque Ville-Marie 75–6, 152; branches 17,18, 56, 59; and English capital 29, 58, 60–1; establishment 35; failure 46, 60–2; operations 58–60; suspension of 1879 55–7

Bay Sulphite Company 138–9

Becker and Company 138

Beaudry, Jean-Baptiste 63

Beaudry, Jean-Louis 34, 76

Beauchemin, L.J.O. 104

Béïque, F.L. 105–6, 116–17, 137, 144, 146

Belgo-Canadian Pulp and Paper Company 107

Bernier, Michel 86

Berthierville, Quebec 15

Bienvenu, Tancrède 66–8, 100, 102, 125, 139

Bill 3 130–6, 139

Boas, Feodor 85–6

Boivin, Wilson and Company 105

Bosworth, G.M. 103–4

Bourassa, Henri 132, 135
Bousquet, J.S. 48–51
Bruchési, Archibishop Paul 74
Burland, G.B. 103–4

Caisse d'Economie de Notre
  Dame de Québec 31–2
caisses populaires 19, 108, 116,
  120, 140, 142; as competition for
  French banks 98, 111–12
Calgary and Edmonton
  Railway 105
Canadian Bankers' Association 7,
  98–9, 123–7, 129; role in suspension of Banque de St-
  Hyacinthe 88–90
Canadian Coloured Cotton 106
Canadian Pacific Railway 105
Canadian Woollen Mills 86
Cannon, J.G. 86
Carsley, Samuel 103–4
Cartier, George-Etienne 143
Cassidy, J.L. 35, 63–4
chartered banks (see also French
  banks, English banks, and
  names of individual banks) 6,
  23, 26, 141–2, 152; branch
  system 4, 6–9, 41, 123;
  competition 4, 23, 78;
  concentration 4, 6, 46, 78–9,
  97, 110, 117, 119–21, 147;
  double liability clause 23, 39;
  linguistically fragmented capital
  market 9, 18, 21; liquidity 52–
  4, 66–7, 133–4, 145–6; note
  circulation 26, 59, 111; struc-

ture of assets and liabilities 4,
  10, 122, 145
Cherrier, C.S. 47
Chicoutimi Pulp Company 107,
  118, 138
Chinic, Eugène 32, 45
City Bank 24, 46
Clouston, Edward 89–90
Compagnie Manufacturière de
  Montmagny 113–14
Compagnie Manufacturière de St-
  Hyacinthe 42, 85
Consolidated Bank 56, 61
Cotté, Honoré 62–3

Daoust, Emilien 104
de Boucherville, George 41
Desjardins, Alphonse (founder of
  caisses populaires) 19, 112, 142
Desjardins, Alphonse (president
  of Banque Jacques-Cartier) 65,
  67, 76, 143
des Rivières, Henri 126
Dessaulles, Georges-Casimir 42–
  3, 85, 87, 92–3, 143
DeWitt, Jacob 26
DeWitt, Viger and Company (see
  also Banque du Peuple) 25–8
Dominion Iron and Steel 102
Dominion Textiles 106
Drayton, Henry 123
Dubuc, J.E.A. 107
Ducharme, G.N. 68, 117
Dumesnil, G.N. 56

Eastern Townships Bank 79–80,
  144, 147; acquisition by Bank of

Commerce 95–6; branches 10–11; establishment 37; operations 67, 89, 91–5

East Richelieu Valley Railway 82

English banks (*see also* names of individual banks): branches in Quebec 10–16, 97, 140; and French clients 14, 146–7; and French directors 23

Exchange Bank of Canada 35, 46, 56, 60

Exchange Bank of Yarmouth 4

Farwell, William 94

Fielding, W.S. 61, 123–4, 126–7, 129

Forget, Rodolphe 102, 144

Fortier, J.H. 125

French banks (*see also* names of individual banks) 120–1, 141; branches 16–21, 75, 98–9, 139; and capital market 12, 17–18; competition with caisses populaires 19; directors 143–4; and English investment 30, 142; and English market 9, 19–20, 70–1, 147; establishment 29, 32; and French capital 30, 47, 71, 75–7, 96, 98–9, 117, 140, 142, 147; operations 75, 98–9, 116, 145; subagencies 20, 98, 112

French businessmen: as seen by historians 22, 147

Gaboury, Auguste 70

Garand, Ubald 58

Garneau, Sir Georges 126

Gault, A.F. 74, 106

Gibb, Joseph 33

Gouin, Sir Lomer 16, 123–9 passim

Granite Mills 85–6

Grenier, Jacques 49, 76

Groulx, Abbé Lionel 97, 121, 137

Hart, Moses 43

Heneker, R.W. 92–3

Holt, Herbert 105

Home Bank 119, 129, 131, 152

Humboldt, Saskatchewan 109

Ingersoll, Ontario 13

Inspector General of Banks 152.

Jackson, Henry 64

Jodoin, Pierre 45

Joseph, Abraham 33

Knight, John 88–90

Lachute, Quebec 18

Laflèche, Saskatchewan 109

Laporte, Hormisdas 103–4, 117, 136

Laporte, Martin et Compagnie 104

Lavoie, Napoléon 111–12, 114–16, 122–3, 126, 139

Leman, Beaudry 106, 108, 125, 136–7, 139

Lemoine, B.H. 28

L'Epiphanie, Quebec 18

Lévis, Quebec 7, 13, 19, 111

Librairie Beauchemin 104
Lichtenheim, Edward 58
La Ligue de protection des
    épargnes de la province de
    Québec 138–9
Louiseville, Quebec 18

Macdonald, Duncan 63
Machine Agricole Nationale
    Limitée 113, 115, 123–5, 132–3,
    138
Macmillan, Senator Donald 50, 54
Maple Leaf Milling 102
Marieville, Quebec 61
Mechanics Bank 35, 46, 56, 75
Merchants' Bank 120, 144;
    branches 11, 42; and French
    clients 14–15
Metropolitan Bank 35, 46, 56, 60
Miner, S.H.C. 94
Molleur, Louis 38, 82–3
Molson, J.H.R. 74
Molson's Bank 11, 120, 138, 144
Monet, Dominique 54
Montmagny, Quebec 111
Montreal City and District
    Savings Bank 31, 74
Montreal Colonization
    Railway 63
Montreal Light, Heat and
    Power 105
Morin, Eusèbe 88
Morrice, David 106

Nicol, Jacob 126
North Star Mining 105

Ontario Bank 4, 78
Ottawa Light, Heat and
    Power 102

Papineauville, Quebec 104
Paquet, Charles 113–15, 118, 128
Paton Manufacturing Company
    92–3
People's Bank of Halifax 10
Philie, L.F. 88–9
Pictou Bank 78
Pomroy, Benjamin 92
P.P. Martin et Compagnie 107
Pratte, Joseph 98
Prendergast, Marie-Joseph-
    Alfred 72, 74
Price, H.M. 71

Quebec: general economic
    situation 12–14, 98
Quebec Bank 23, 33, 75, 110, 147;
    branches 43–4; French
    directors 23
Quebec City: decline as banking
    centre 110
Quebec Southern Railway 87, 90

Rainville, J.H. 89–91
Regent Securities Company 106
Regina Shoe Company 107
Rivière-du-Loup, Quebec 98
Robitaille, Olivier 31–3
Rodier, C.S. 63
Roy, P.H. 81–3
Royal Bank 102, 110, 120

Saguenay Pulp and Power
    Company 107, 138–9

St-Césaire, Quebec 14, 88, 90
St-Charles, F.X. 73
St-Cuthbert, Quebec 56
St-Hyacinthe, Quebec 9, 13, 41,
 84–6
St-Jacques, Romuald 42–3
St-Jean, Quebec 37, 80
St-Rémi, Quebec 13, 54, 81, 84
Sauvé, Arthur 135
La Sauvegarde 117
savings banks 31
Séguin, Lalime et Compagnie 55,
 85–6
Shawinigan Cotton 106
Sherbrooke, Quebec 92–3
Société d'Administration
 Générale 116
Société de Construction de
 Montmagny 114
société en commandite 27–9
Société Permanente de Construc-
 tion du District d'Iberville 39
Société Permanente de Construc-
 tion d'Yamaska 42
Stadacona Bank 33, 46, 75
Stephen, George 93

Taschereau, C.E. 126
Taschereau, Louis-Alexandre (see
 also Bill 3) 125–7, 130–2, 134–6,
 140
Tessier, Ulric 32
Thibaudeau, Joseph 70
Thomson, D.C. 33

Three Rivers Lumber
 Company 107
Transportation and Shipping
 Company 115, 124
Trois-Rivières, Quebec 56, 79
Trottier, A.A. 47
Trudeau, Romuald 34
Trust Général 116
Tupper, Charles 54
Turner, Richard 71

Union Bank of Lower Canada 33,
 44, 75, 104, 110, 147
United Counties Railway 86
Usines Générales de Chars et de
 Machineries 114

Vaillancourt, J.A. 139
Vallée, Prudent 129
Valois, Louis-Etienne Avila 36
Vanier, Anatole 137
Viger, Louis-Michel 26, 76

Wabasso Cotton 106
Wayagamack Pulp and Paper
 Company 106
Weir, William 18, 57–60, 64, 82
Western Bank 78
Weyburn Security Bank 6
Whitehead, C.R. 106
Wilkie, D.P. 90
Wilson, Joseph-Marcellin 105,
 107, 117, 157
Windsor Mills, Quebec 18
Withall, W.J. 58

The Social History of Canada

General Editors:
Michael Bliss 1971–7
H.V. Nelles 1978–

1 **The Wretched of Canada:**
Letters to R.B. Bennett 1930–1935
Edited and introduced by
L.M. Grayson and Michael Bliss

2 **Canada and the Canadian
Question**
Goldwin Smith
Introduction, Carl Berger

3 **My Neighbor**
J.S. Woodsworth
Introduction, Richard Allen

4 **The Bunkhouse Man**
E.W. Bradwin
Introduction, Jean Burnet

5 **In Times Like These**
Nellie McClung
Introduction, Veronica Strong-
Boag

6 **The City below the Hill**
Herbert Brown Ames
Introduction, Paul Rutherford

7 **Strangers within Our Gates**
J.S. Woodsworth
Introduction, Marilyn Barber

8 **The Rapids**
Alan Sullivan
Introduction, Michael Bliss

9 **Philosophy of Railroads
and Other Essays**
T.C. Keefer
Introduction, H.V. Nelles

10 **The Americanization of
Canada 1907**
Samuel E. Moffett
Introduction, Allan Smith

11 **Rural Life in Canada:**
Its Trend and Tasks
John MacDougall
Introduction, R. Craig Brown

12 **The New Christianity**
Salem Bland
Introduction, Richard Allen

13 **Canada Investigates
Industrialism:**
The Royal Commission on the
Relations of Labor and Capital
Edited and introduced by
Greg Kealey

14 **Industry and Humanity**
William Lyon Mackenzie King
Introduction, David Jay Bercuson

15 **The Social Criticism of
Stephen Leacock:**
The Unsolved Riddle of Social
Justice and Other Essays
Stephen Leacock
Edited and introduced by
Alan Bowker

16 **A Dutch Homesteader on
the Prairies:**
The Letters of Willem de Gelder
Translated and introduced by
H. Ganzevoort

17 **The Tragedy of Quebec:**
The Expulsion of its Protestant
Farmers
Robert Sellar
Introduction, Robert Hill

18 The Woman Suffrage Movement
in Canada
Catherine L. Cleverdon
Introduction, Ramsay Cook

19 The Queen v Louis Riel
Introduction, Desmond Morton

20 The Writing on the Wall
Hilda Glynn-Ward
Introduction, Patricia E. Roy

21 By Great Waters:
A Newfoundland and Labrador
Anthology
Edited and introduced by Peter
Neary and Patrick O'Flaherty

22 Saving the Canadian City.
The First Phase 1880–1920:
An Anthology of Early Articles on
Urban Reform
Edited and introduced by
Paul Rutherford

23 The Magpie
Douglas Durkin
Introduction, Peter E. Rider

24 Report on Social Security
for Canada
Leonard Marsh
New introduction by the author

25 A History of Farmers'
Movements in Canada
Louis Aubrey Wood
Introduction, Foster J.K. Griezic

26 Social Planning for Canada
League for Social Reconstruction
Introduction, F.R. Scott, Leonard
Marsh, Graham Spry, J. King
Gordon, E.A. Forsey, and J.F.
Parkinson

27 For My Country (Pour la patrie)
Jules-Paul Tardivel
Translation, Sheila Fischman
Introduction, A.I. Silver

28 The Politics of Labor
T. Phillips Thompson
Introduction, Jay Atherton

29 The Land of Open Doors
Being Letters from Western
Canada 1911–13
J. Burgon Bickersteth
New Introduction by the author

30 Wheat and Woman
Georgina Binnie-Clark
Introduction, Susan Jackel

31 A Darkened House:
Cholera in Nineteenth-Century
Canada
Geoffrey Bilson

32 'A Woman with a Purpose'
The Diaries of Elizabeth Smith
1872–1884
Edited and introduced by Veronica
Strong-Boag

33 Within the Barbed Wire Fence
A Japanese Man's Account of His
Internment in Canada
Takeo Ujo Nakano with Leatrice
Nakano
Afterword by W. Peter Ward

34 Confessions of an
Immigrant's Daughter
Laura Goodman Salverson
Introduction, K.P. Stich

35 But This Is Our War
Grace Morris Craig

36 Jack in Port
Sailortowns of Eastern Canada
Judith Fingard

37 Liberation Deferred?
The Ideas of the English-Canadian
Suffragists, 1877–1918
Carol Lee Bacchi

38 Banking en français:
The French Banks of Quebec,
1835–1925
Ronald Rudin